VOLUME 5

DELUXE
GUITAR
PLAY-ALONG

AUDIO ACCESS INCLUDED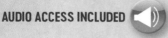

blues standards

C000285324

PLAYBACK+
Speed • Pitch • Balance • Loop

To access audio visit:
www.halleonard.com/mylibrary

"Enter Code"
2732-9874-1546-5430

ISBN 978-1-5400-0374-4

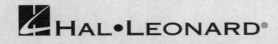

HAL•LEONARD®

Visit Hal Leonard Online at
www.halleonard.com

Contact Us:
Hal Leonard
7777 West Bluemound Road
Milwaukee, WI 53213
Email: info@halleonard.com

In Europe contact:
Hal Leonard Europe Limited
42 Wigmore Street
Marylebone, London, W1U 2RN
Email: info@halleonardeurope.com

In Australia contact:
Hal Leonard Australia Pty. Ltd.
4 Lentara Court
Cheltenham, Victoria, 3192 Australia
Email: info@halleonard.com.au

blues standards

GUITAR NOTATION LEGEND

THE MUSICAL STAFF shows pitches and rhythms and is divided by bar lines into measures. Pitches are named after the first seven letters of the alphabet.

TABLATURE graphically represents the guitar fingerboard. Each horizontal line represents a string, and each number represents a fret.

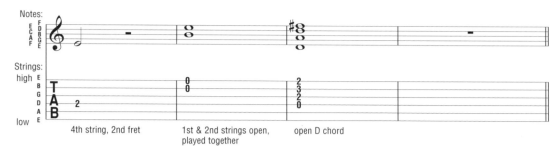

4th string, 2nd fret   1st & 2nd strings open, played together   open D chord

HALF-STEP BEND: Strike the note and bend up 1/2 step.

WHOLE-STEP BEND: Strike the note and bend up one step.

GRACE NOTE BEND: Strike the note and immediately bend up as indicated.

SLIGHT (MICROTONE) BEND: Strike the note and bend up 1/4 step.

BEND AND RELEASE: Strike the note and bend up as indicated, then release back to the original note. Only the first note is struck.

PRE-BEND: Bend the note as indicated, then strike it.

VIBRATO: The string is vibrated by rapidly bending and releasing the note with the fretting hand.

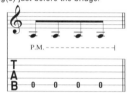

PALM MUTING: The note is partially muted by the pick hand lightly touching the string(s) just before the bridge.

HAMMER-ON: Strike the first (lower) note with one finger, then sound the higher note (on the same string) with another finger by fretting it without picking.

PULL-OFF: Place both fingers on the notes to be sounded. Strike the first note and without picking, pull the finger off to sound the second (lower) note.

LEGATO SLIDE: Strike the first note and then slide the same fret-hand finger up or down to the second note. The second note is not struck.

SHIFT SLIDE: Same as legato slide, except the second note is struck.

TRILL: Very rapidly alternate between the notes indicated by continuously hammering on and pulling off.

TAPPING: Hammer ("tap") the fret indicated with the pick-hand index or middle finger and pull off to the note fretted by the fret hand.

NATURAL HARMONIC: Strike the note while the fret-hand lightly touches the string directly over the fret indicated.

PINCH HARMONIC: The note is fretted normally and a harmonic is produced by adding the edge of the thumb or the tip of the index finger of the pick hand to the normal pick attack.

TREMOLO PICKING: The note is picked as rapidly and continuously as possible.

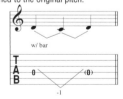

VIBRATO BAR DIVE AND RETURN: The pitch of the note or chord is dropped a specified number of steps (in rhythm), then returned to the original pitch.

VIBRATO BAR SCOOP: Depress the bar just before striking the note, then quickly release the bar.

VIBRATO BAR DIP: Strike the note and then immediately drop a specified number of steps, then release back to the original pitch.

Additional Musical Definitions

 (accent) • Accentuate note (play it louder).

 (staccato) • Play the note short.

D.S. al Coda • Go back to the sign (§), then play until the measure marked "*To Coda*," then skip to the section labelled "**Coda**."

D.C. al Fine • Go back to the beginning of the song and play until the measure marked "*Fine*" (end).

Fill

N.C.

• Label used to identify a brief melodic figure which is to be inserted into the arrangement.

• Harmony is implied.

• Repeat measures between signs.

• When a repeated section has different endings, play the first ending only the first time and the second ending only the second time.

Baby, What You Want Me to Do

Words and Music by Jimmy Reed

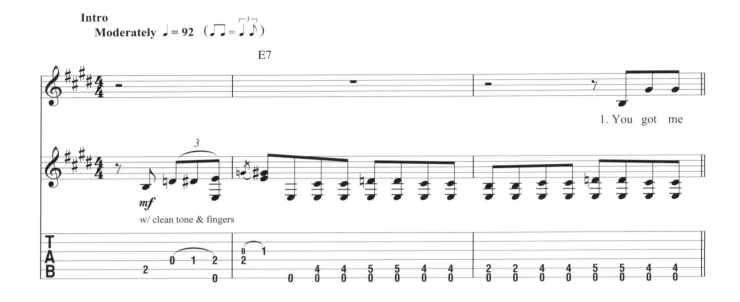

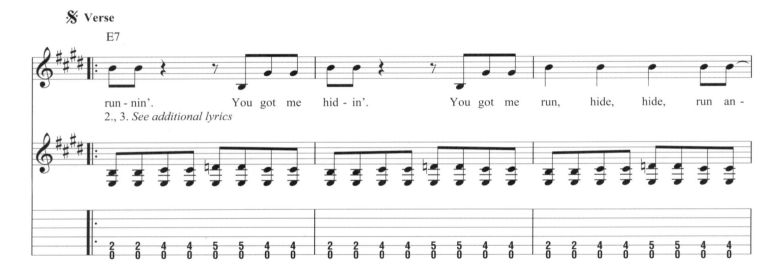

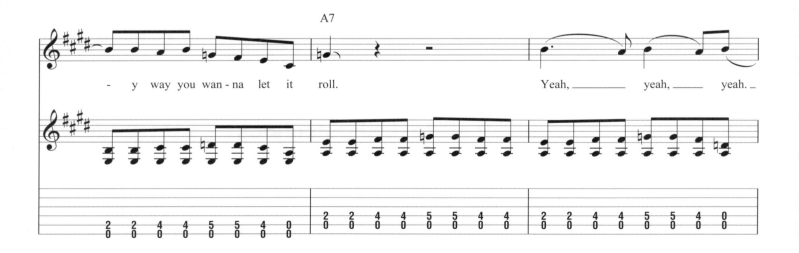

You got me doin' what you want me, but

ba - by, why you wan-na let go?

2. Go - in'

Harmonica Solo

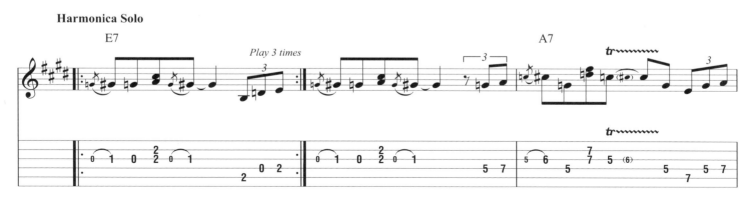

Additional Lyrics

2. Goin' up. Goin' down.
   Goin' up, down, down, up, any way you wanna let it roll.
   Yeah, yeah, yeah.
   You got me doin' what you want me,
   But baby, why you wanna let go?

3. You got me peepin'. You got me hidin'.
   You got me peep, hide, hide, peep, any way you wanna let it roll.
   Yeah, yeah, yeah.
   You got me doin' what you want me,
   But baby, why you wanna let go?

Double Trouble

Words and Music by Otis Rush

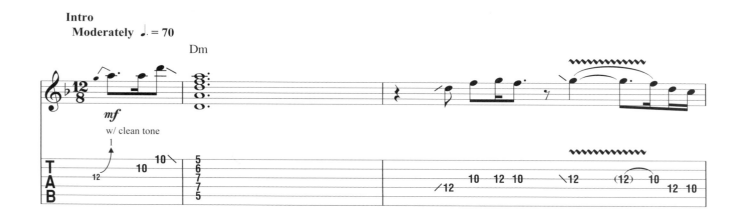

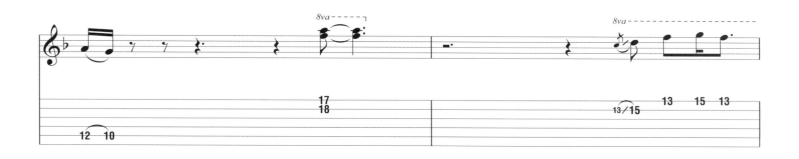

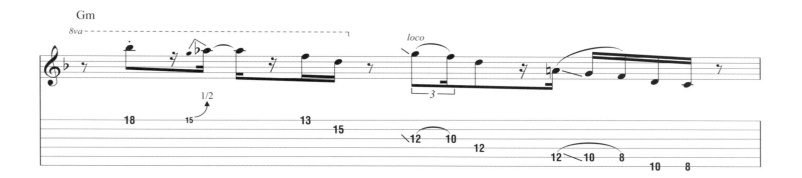

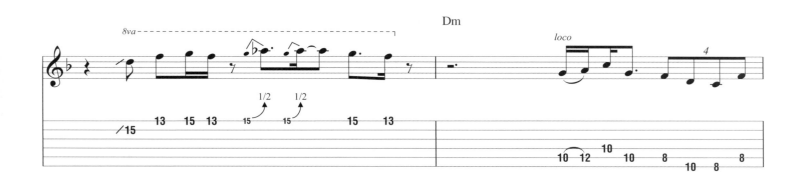

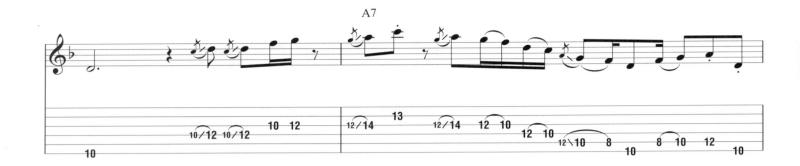

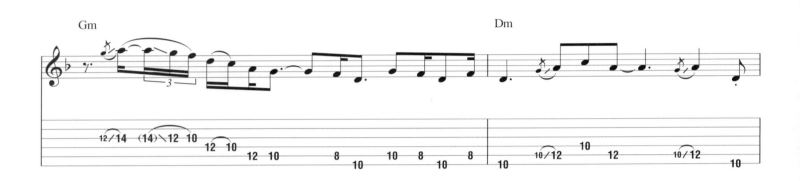

1. I'd lay a-wake at night,___ these thoughts of love,___ and just___ so___

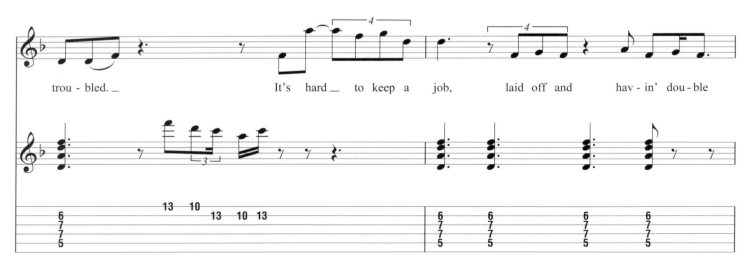

trou - bled. __ It's hard __ to keep a job, laid off and hav - in' dou - ble

trou - ble.   But, hey, hey, _____   yeah, _

they say you can make _ it   if you try.

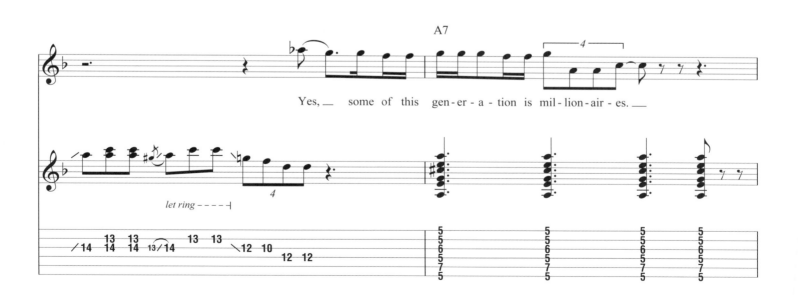

Yes, __ some of this gen - er - a - tion is mil - lion - air - es. __

It's hard _ for me to keep de-cent clothes _ to wear. _

Interlude

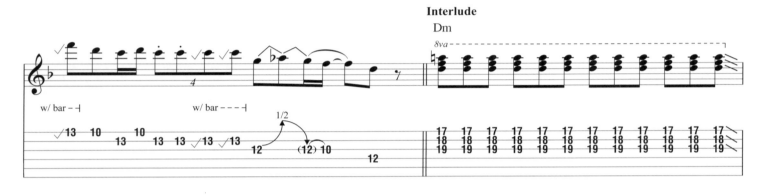

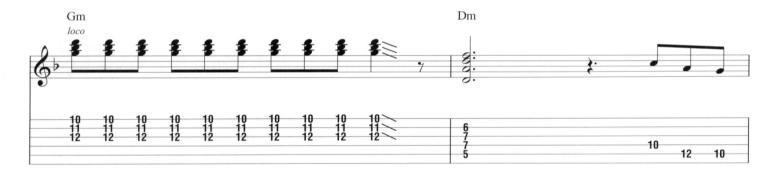

2. You laughed at me walk-in',

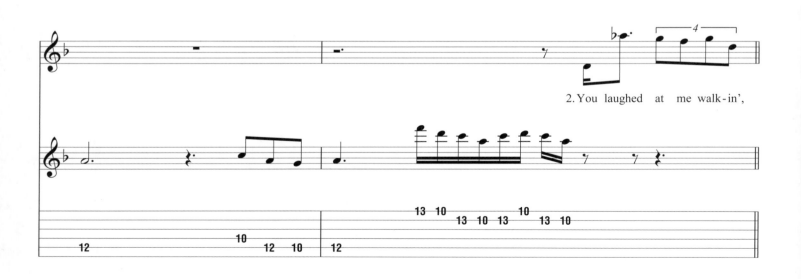

ba - by,   when I had ___   no ___ place _ to   go.

Bad luck and trou - ble tak - en   me, ___   I have   no mon - ey   to show. ___

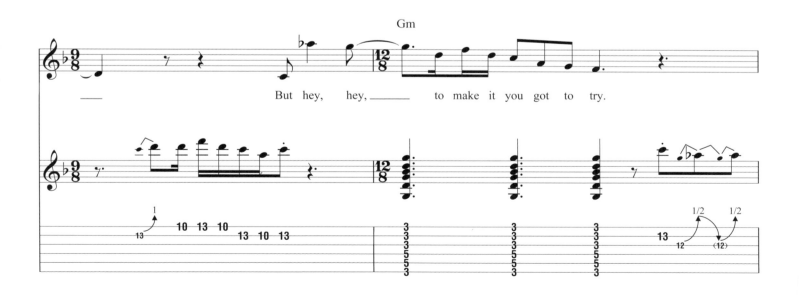

___   But hey,   hey, ___   to make it you got to try.

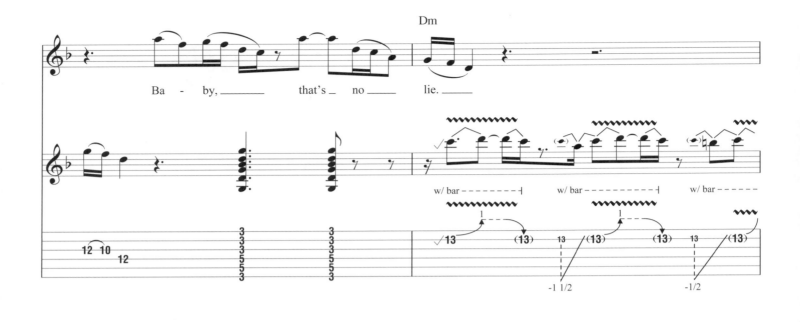

Dm

Ba - by, _____ that's _ no _ lie. _____

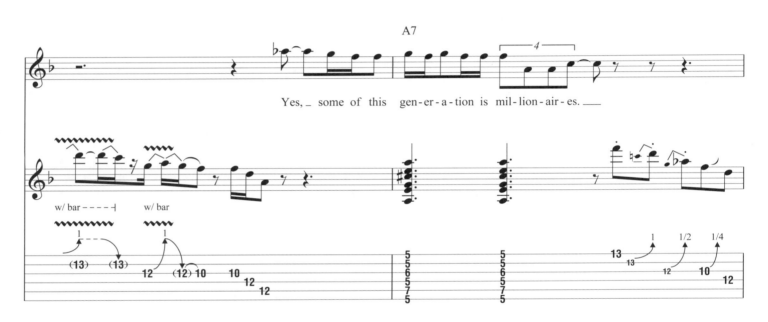

A7

Yes, _ some of this gen-er-a-tion is mil-lion-air-es. _____

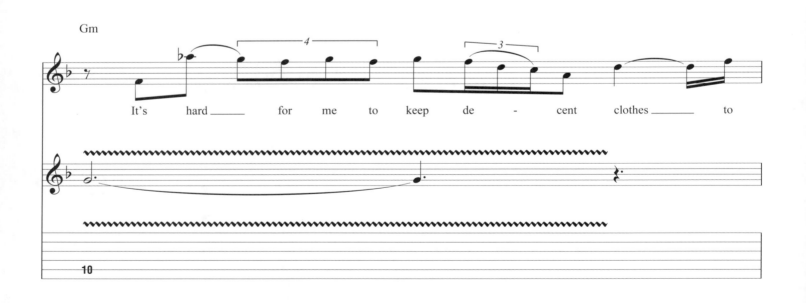

Gm

It's hard _____ for me to keep de - cent clothes _____ to

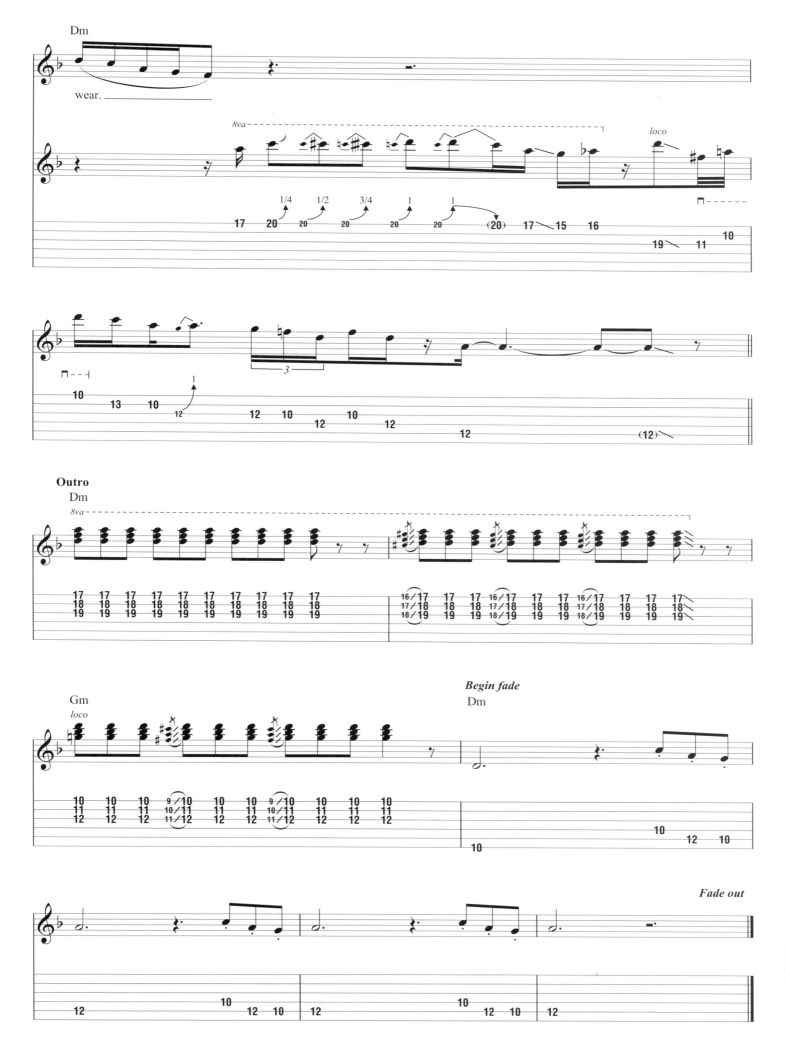

Crosscut Saw

Words and Music by R.G. Ford

Drop D tuning, down 1 1/2 steps:
(low to high) B-F#-B-E-G#-C#

Intro

Moderately ♩ = 122

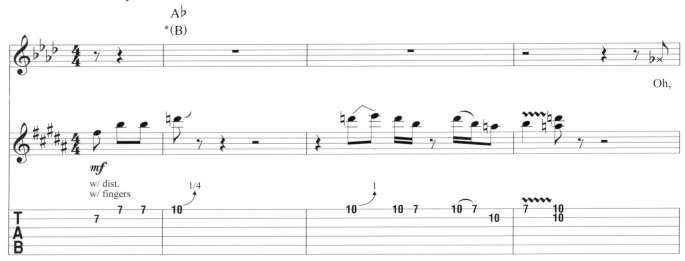

Oh,

*Symbols in parentheses represent chord names respective to detuned guitar.
Symbols above reflect actual sounding chords.

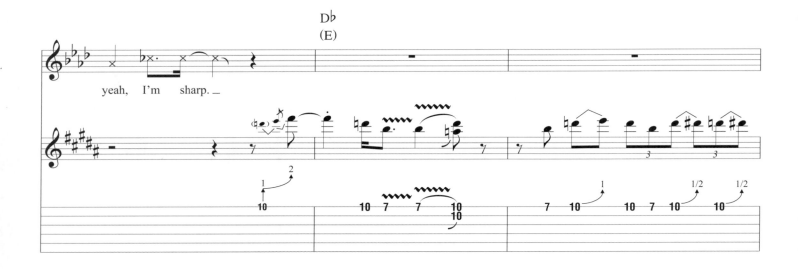

yeah, I'm sharp. ___

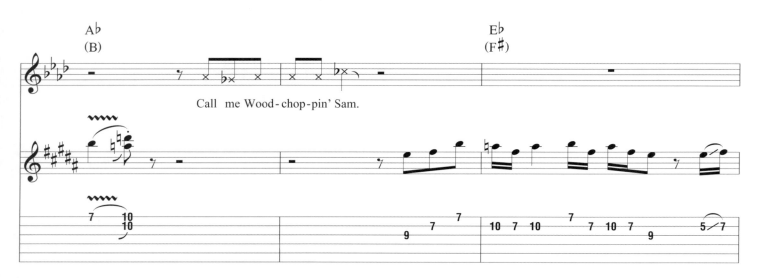

Call me Wood-chop-pin' Sam.

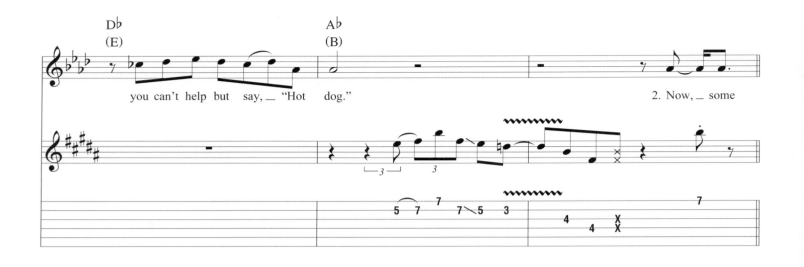

you can't help but say, — "Hot dog."   2. Now, — some

Verse

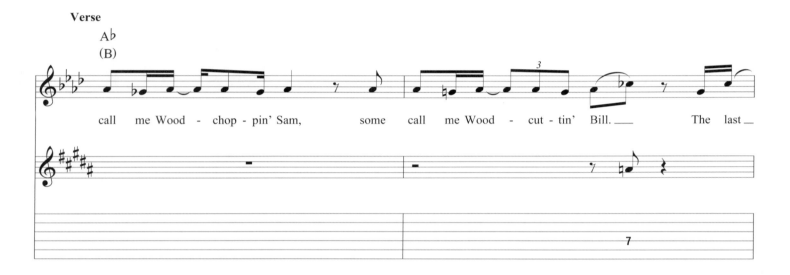

call me Wood - chop - pin' Sam,   some   call   me   Wood - cut - tin'   Bill. __   The   last __

Gtr. tacet

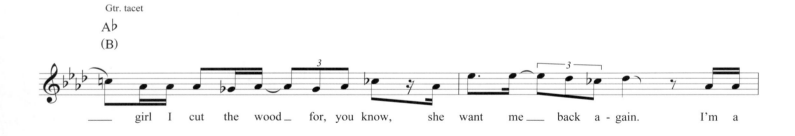

__ girl I cut the wood __ for, you know,   she   want   me __ back a - gain.   I'm a

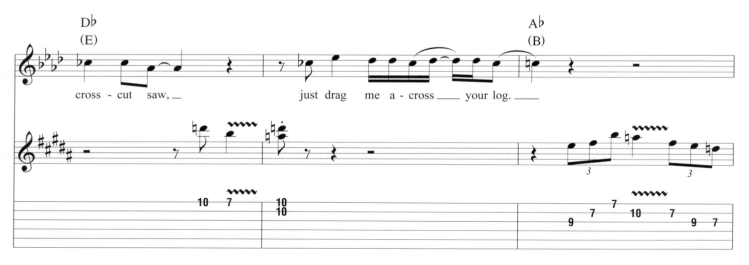

cross - cut saw, __   just drag   me a - cross ___ your log. ___

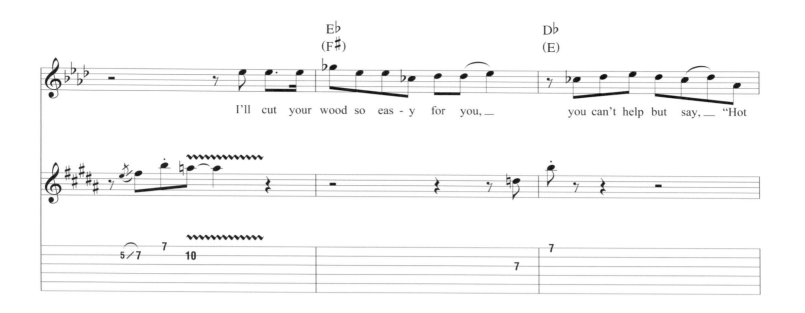

I'll cut your wood so eas - y for you, __ you can't help but say, __ "Hot

Guitar Solo

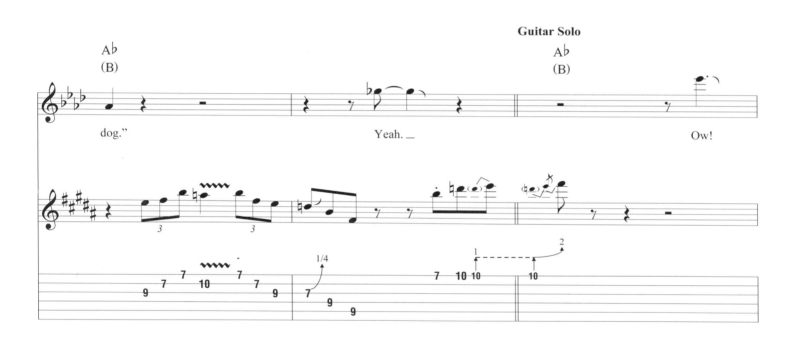

dog." Yeah. __ Ow!

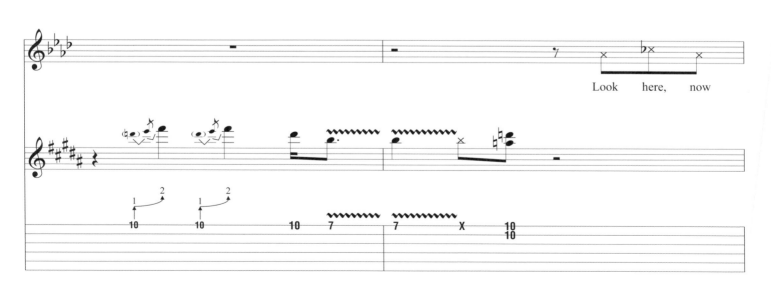

Look here, now

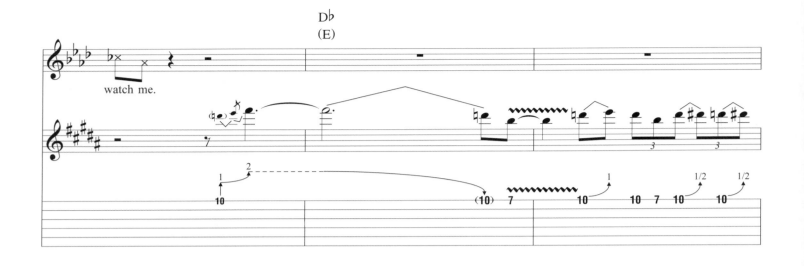

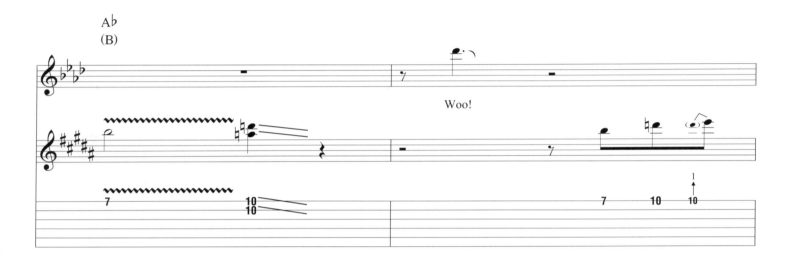

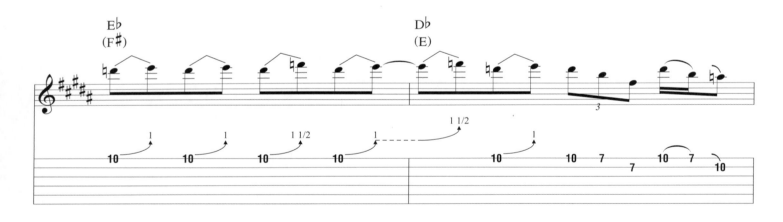

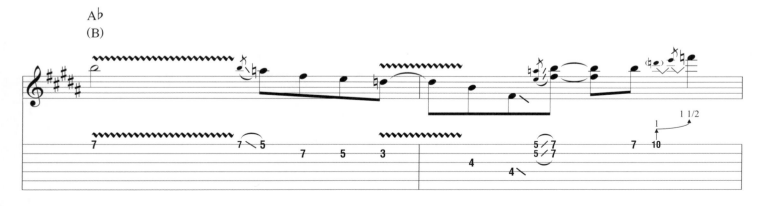

20

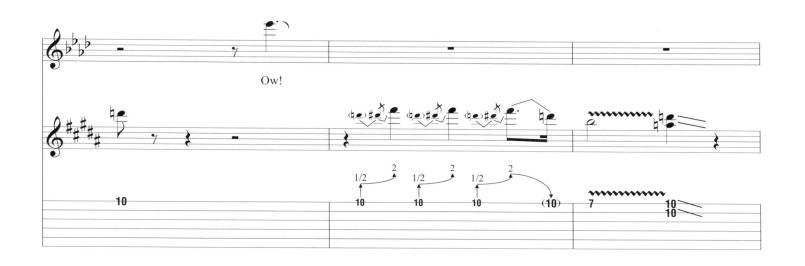

Ow!

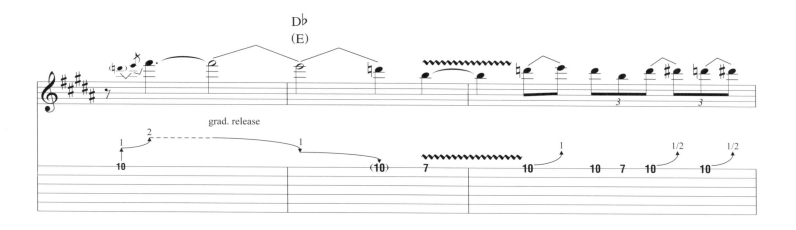

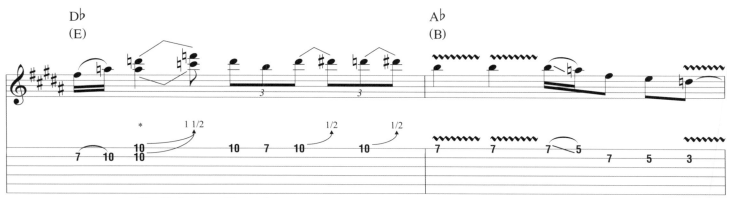

*Bend both strings with same finger.

Verse

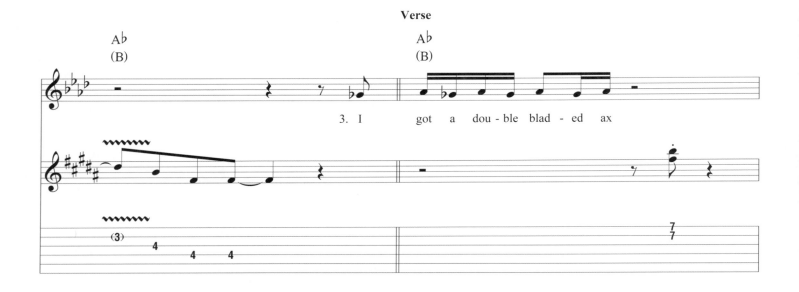

3. I got a dou-ble blad-ed ax

that real-ly cuts good. ___ But I'm a cross - cut saw, just

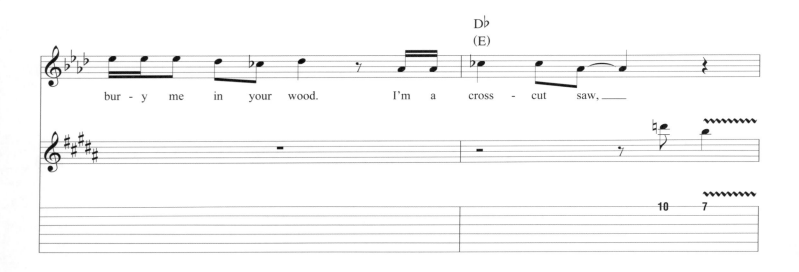

bur-y me in your wood. I'm a cross - cut saw, ___

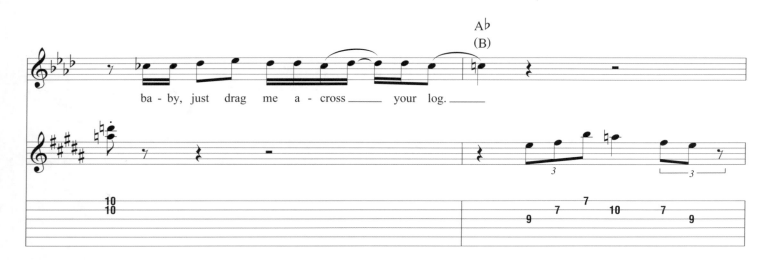

ba - by, just drag me a - cross ___ your log. ___

I'll cut your wood so eas - y for you, wom - an,

you can't help but say, __ "Hot dog."

Now, watch this.

Outro

Begin fade

Fade out

Ow!

Every Day I Have the Blues

Words and Music by Peter Chatman

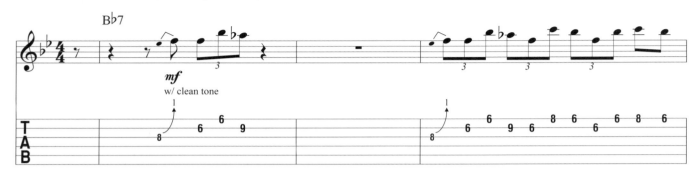

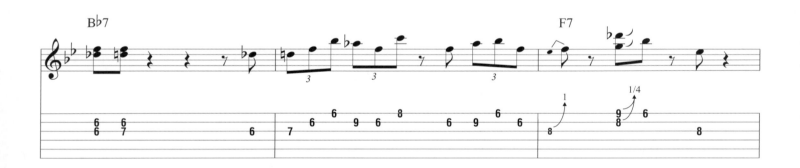

1. Ev - 'ry   day,

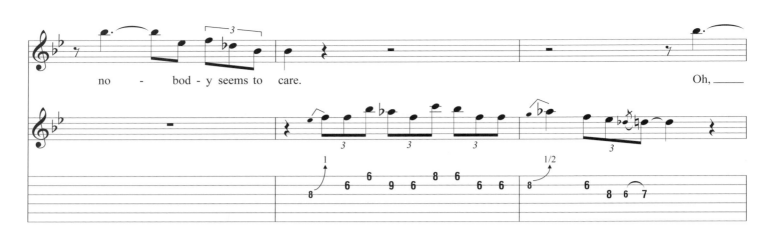

no - bod - y seems to care. Oh, _____

_____ no - bod - y loves _____ me, no - bod - y seems to care.

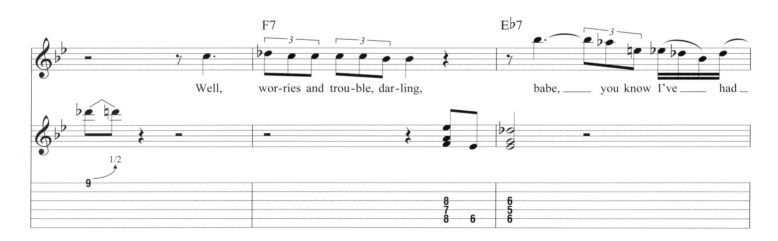

Well, wor-ries and trou-ble, dar-ling, babe, _____ you know I've _____ had _____

Guitar Solo

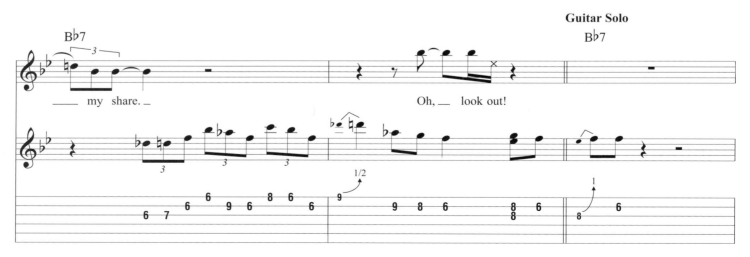

_____ my share. _____ Oh, ___ look out!

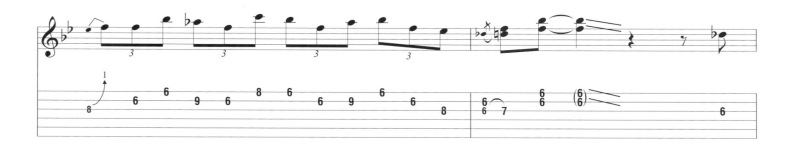

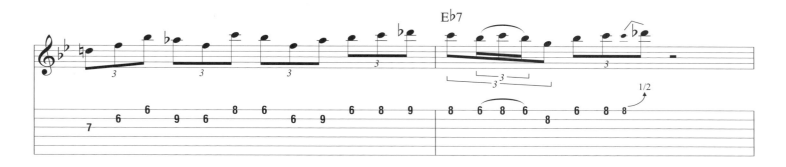

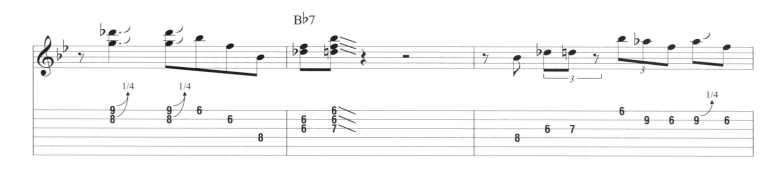

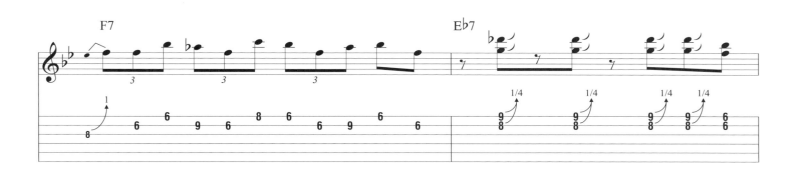

Verse

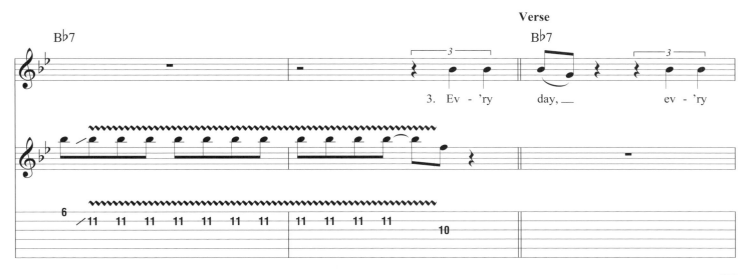

3. Ev - 'ry day, ___ ev - 'ry

day, ___ ev - 'ry day, ev - 'ry day, ev -

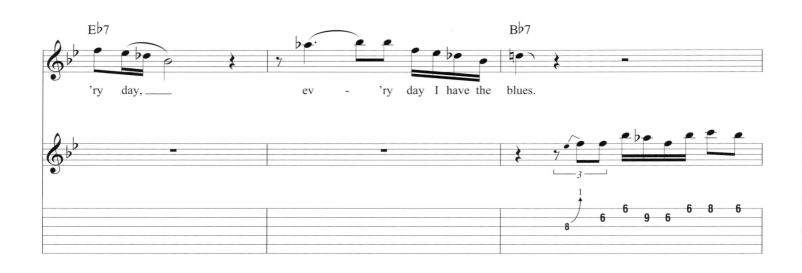

'ry day, ___ ev - 'ry day I have the blues.

When you see me wor-ry-in', babe, ___ babe, ___ it's you I

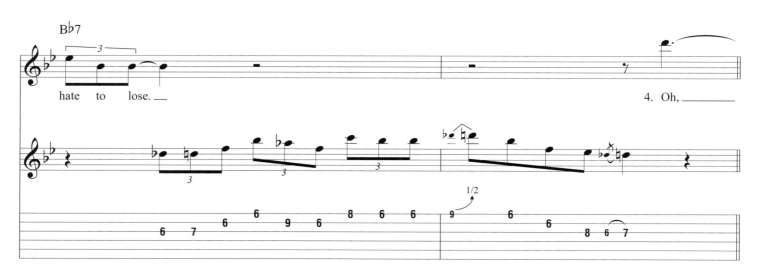

hate to lose. ___ 4. Oh, ___

Going Down

Words and Music by Don Nix

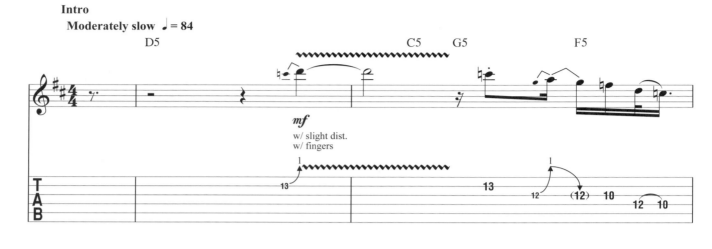

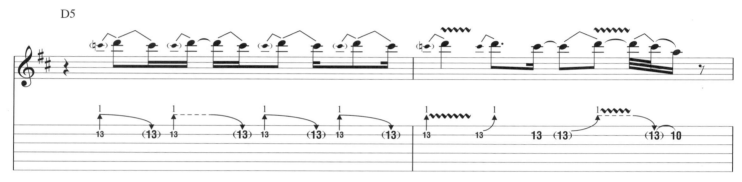

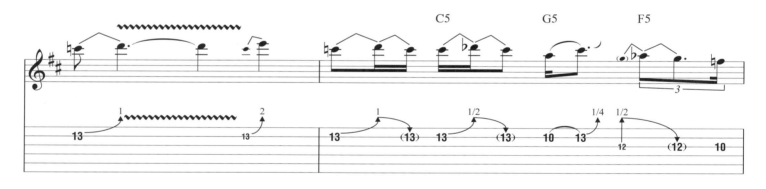

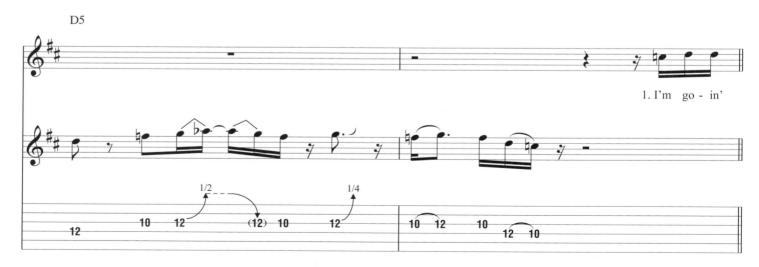

Verse

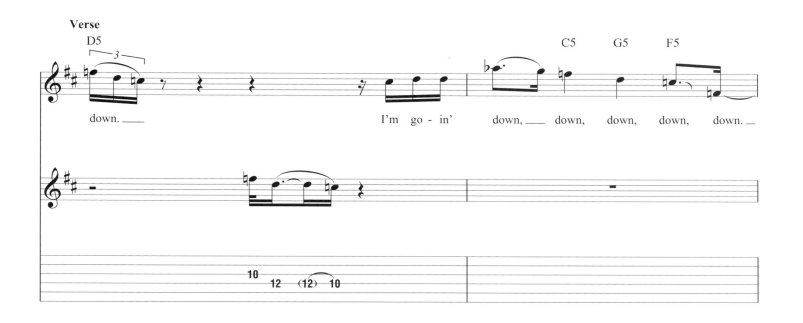

down. _____   I'm go - in'   down, ___ down,   down,   down,   down. __

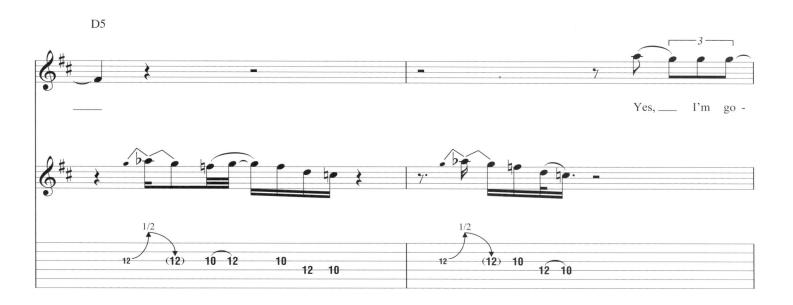

_____   Yes, ___ I'm go -

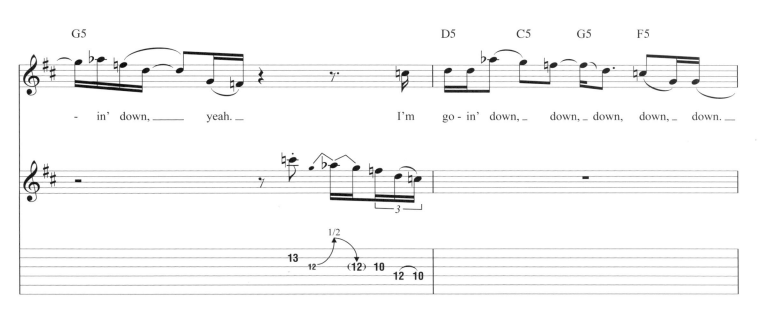

- in' down, ____ yeah. __   I'm   go - in' down, _   down, _ down,   down, _ down. __

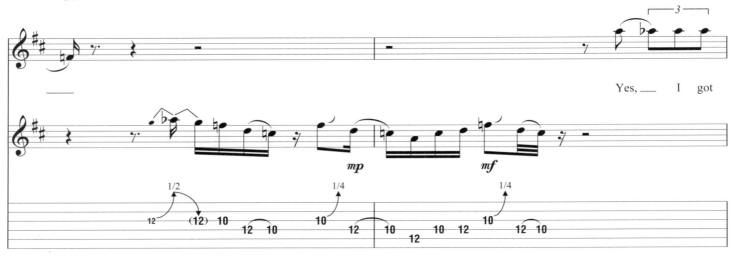

Yes, ___ I got

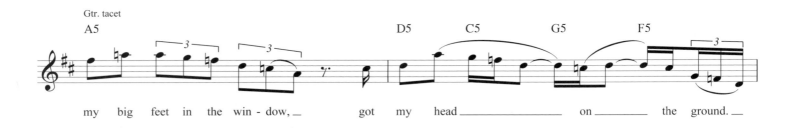

my big feet in the win - dow, ___ got my head ___ on ___ the ground. ___

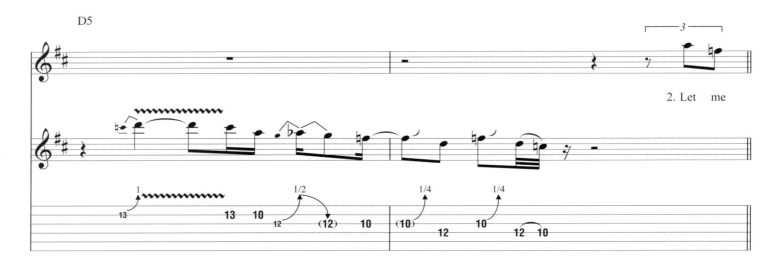

2. Let me

Verse

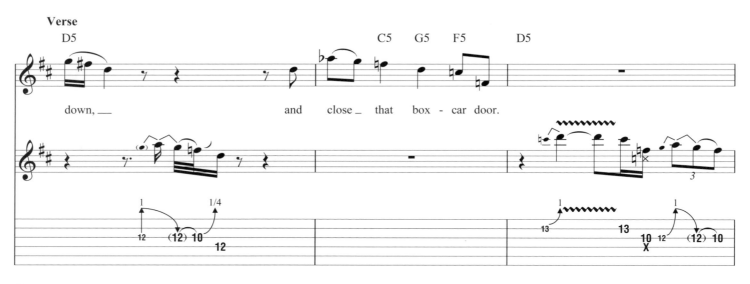

down, ___ and close _ that box - car door.

Yes, ___ let me down, yeah, ___

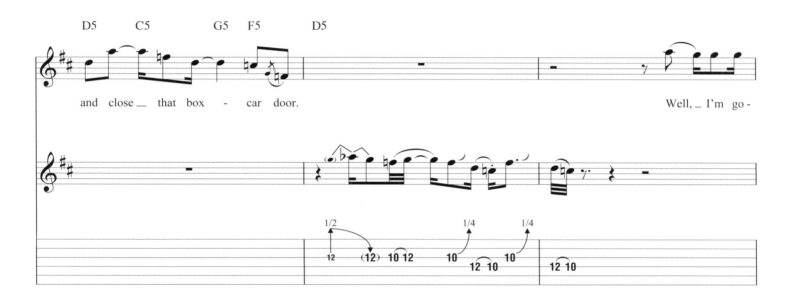

and close __ that box - car door. Well, _ I'm go-

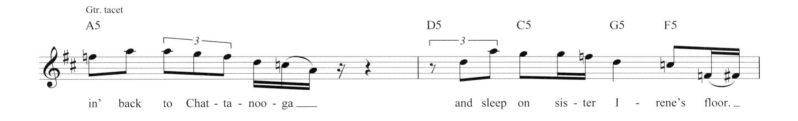

Gtr. tacet

in' back to Chat - ta - noo - ga ___ and sleep on sis - ter I - rene's floor. _

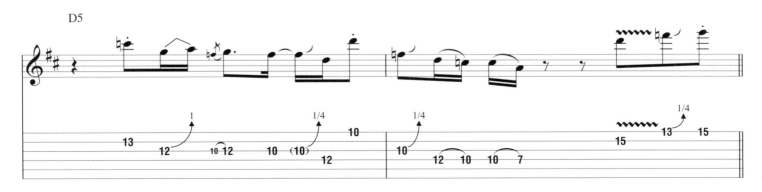

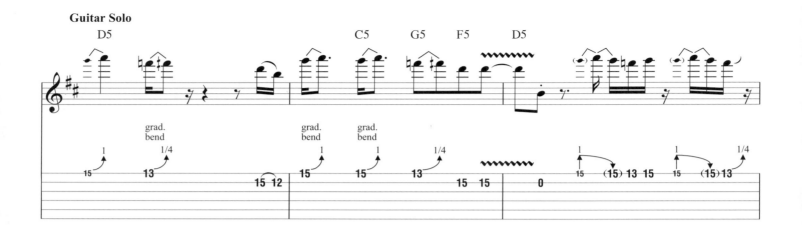

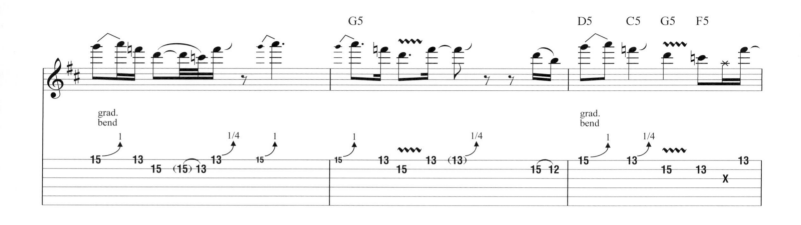

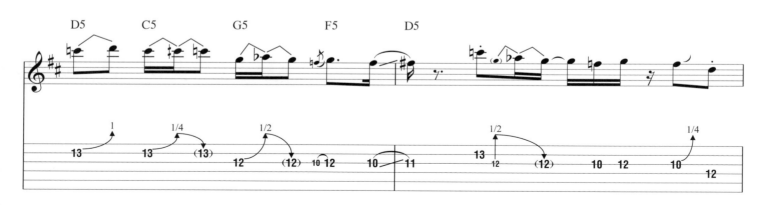

Verse

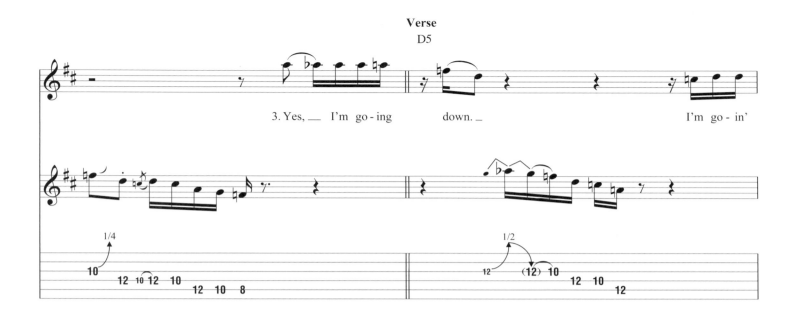

3. Yes, ___ I'm go - ing   down. ___   I'm go - in'

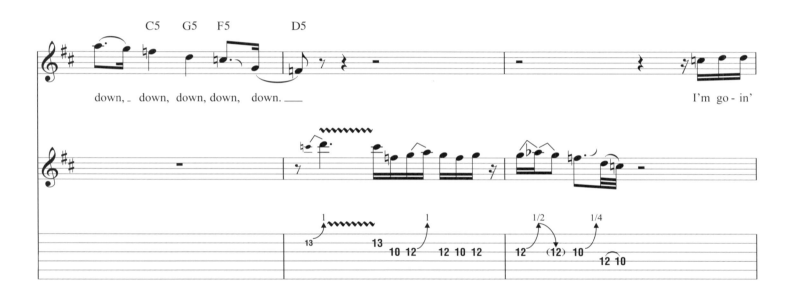

down, _ down, down, down,   down. ___   I'm go - in'

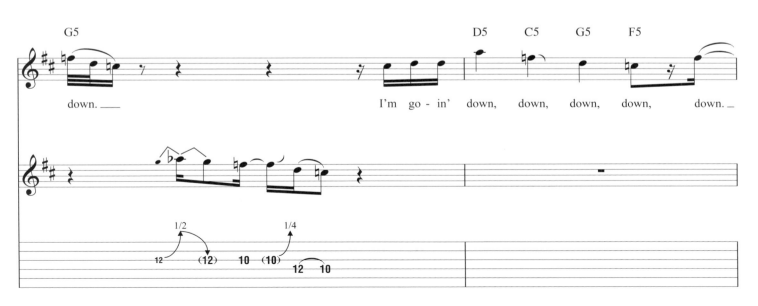

down. ___   I'm go - in' down,   down,   down,   down,   down. _

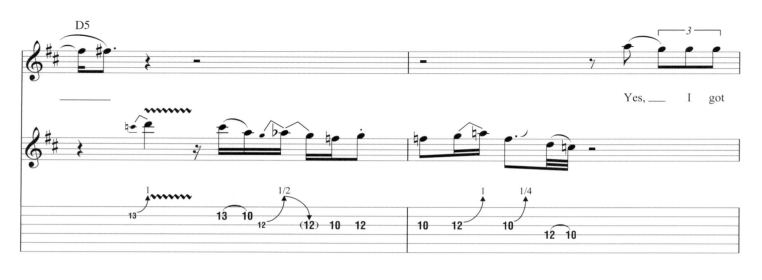

Yes, __ I got

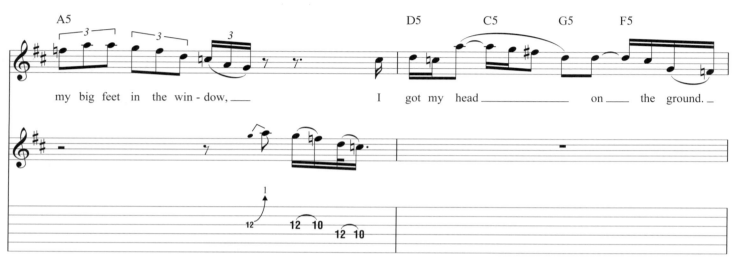

my big feet in the win-dow, __ I got my head _____ on ___ the ground. __

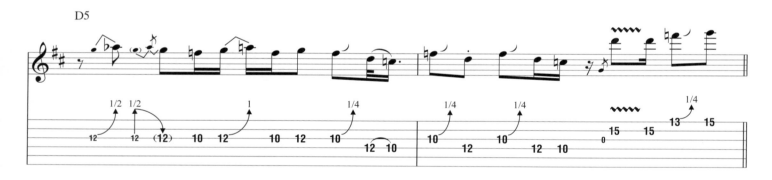

Outro-Guitar Solo

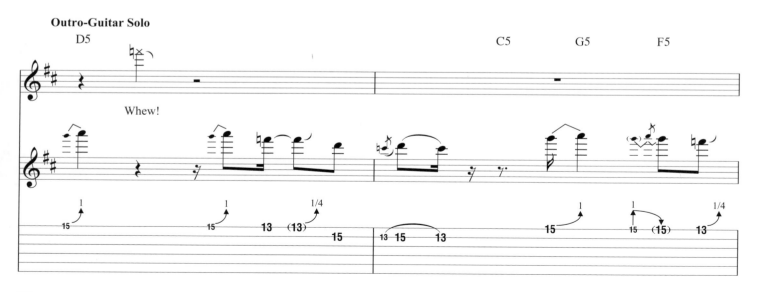

Whew!

36

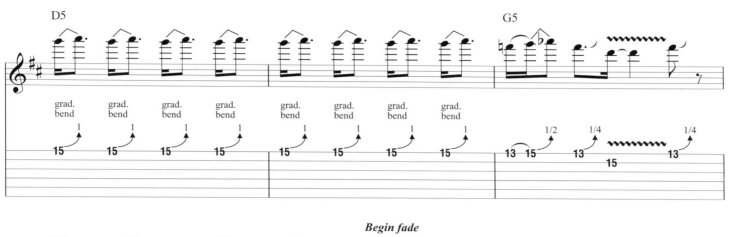

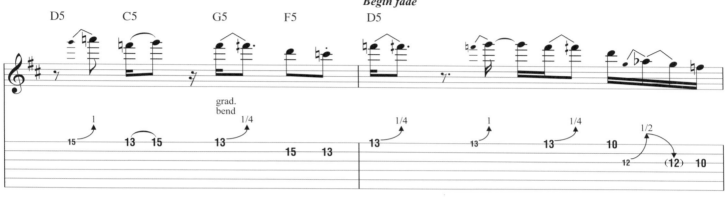

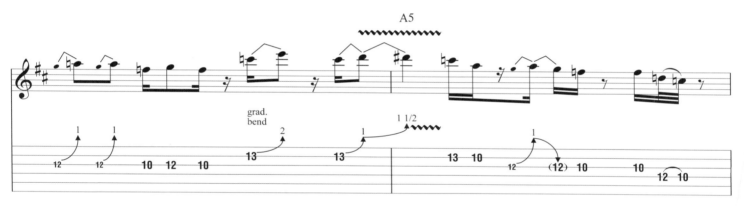

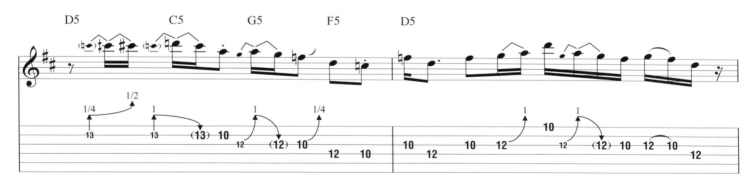

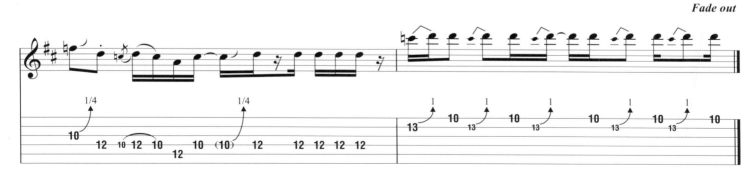

I'm Tore Down

Words and Music by Sonny Thompson

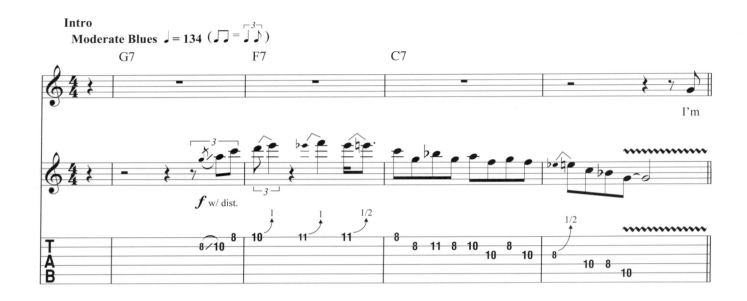

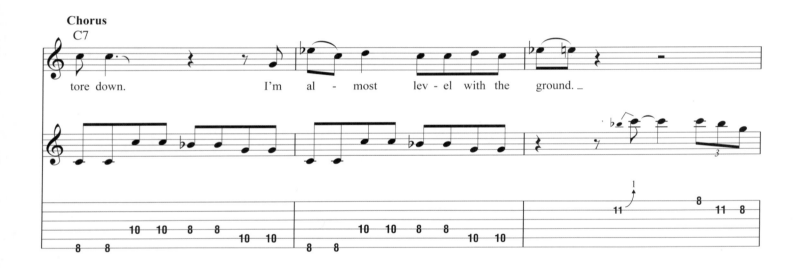

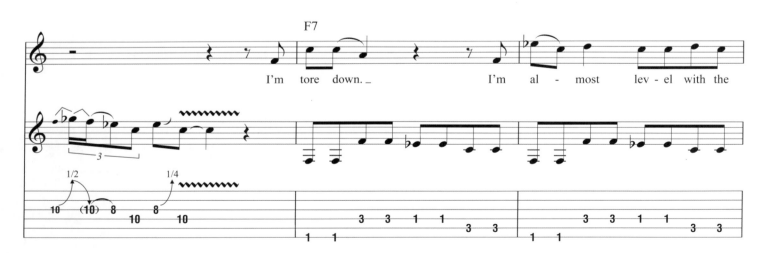

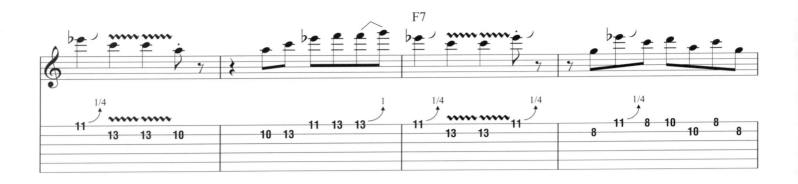

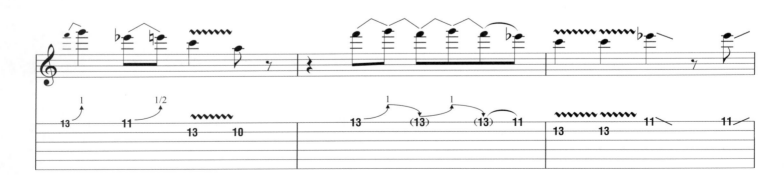

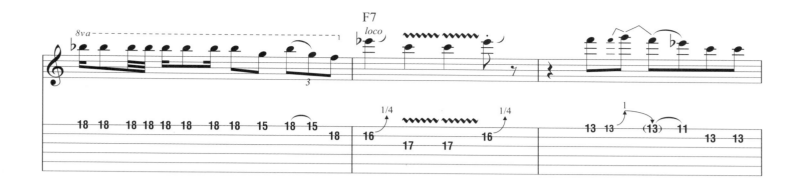

D.S. al Coda

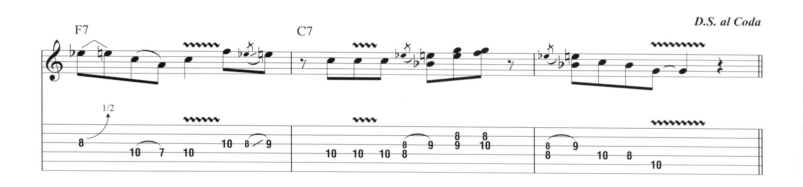

Outro-Chorus

I'm tore down, _____ al - most lev - el with the

Additional Lyrics

3. Love you, baby, with all my might.
Love like mine is outta sight.
I'll lie for you if you want me to.
I really don't believe that your love is true.

Just Your Fool

Words and Music by Walter Jacobs

Verse

your fool, _____ can't help my - self. I love you,

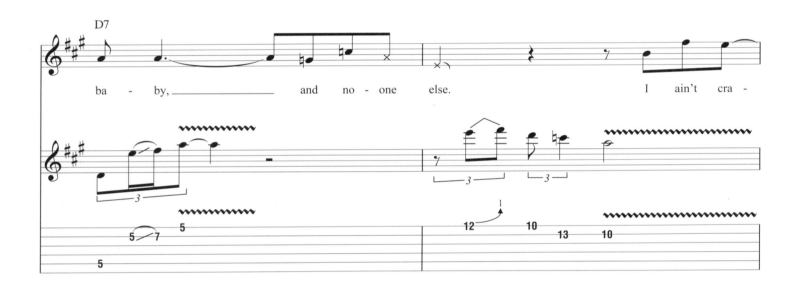

ba - by, _____ and no - one else. I ain't cra -

-zy, _____ you are my ba - by. _____ I'm _____ just

Bridge

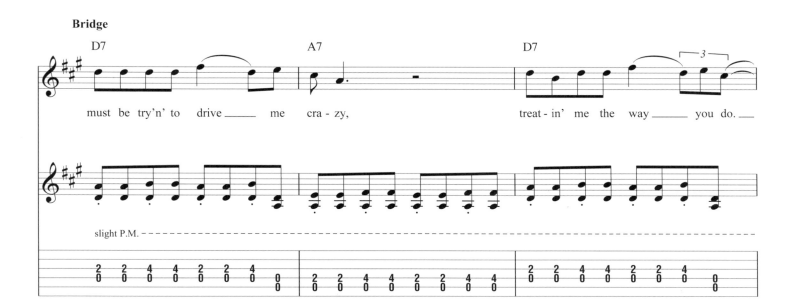

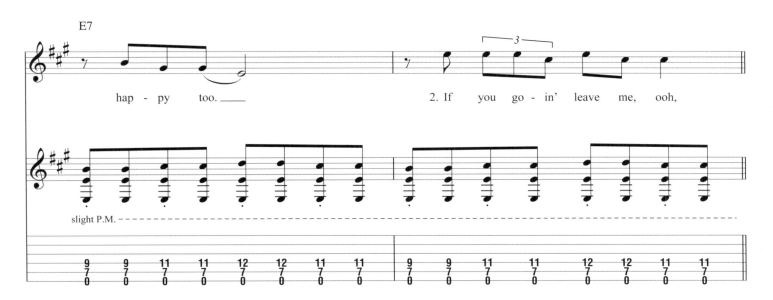

Verse

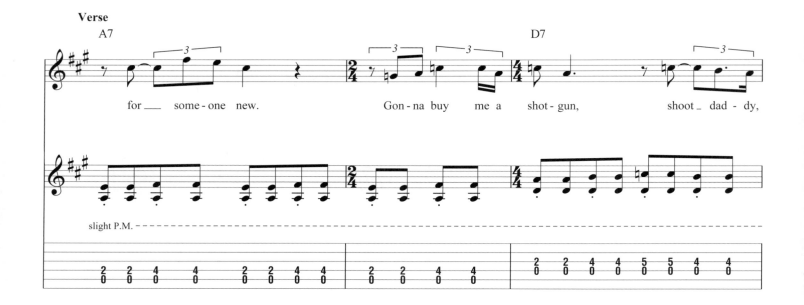

for ___ some-one new. Gon-na buy me a shot-gun, shoot _ dad-dy,

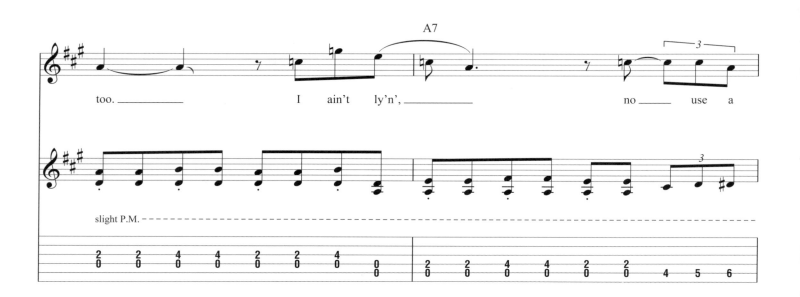

too. _____ I ain't ly'n', _____ no ____ use a

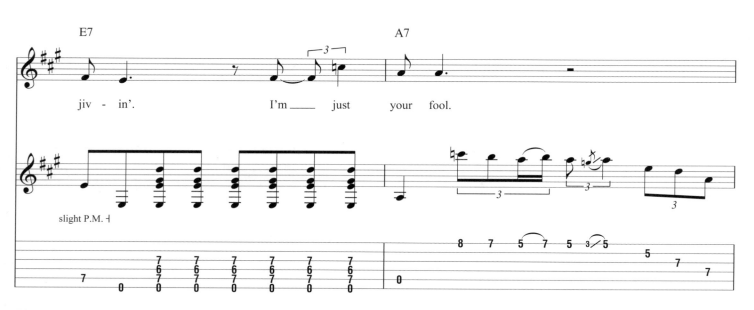

jiv - in'. I'm ___ just your fool.

Outro-Verse

I'm Your Hoochie Coochie Man

Words and Music by Willie Dixon

Intro
Slow Blues ♩. = 75

Verse

A7   A7

1. The gyp-sy wom-an told my moth-er
2., 3. *See additional lyrics*

mf w/ slight dist.

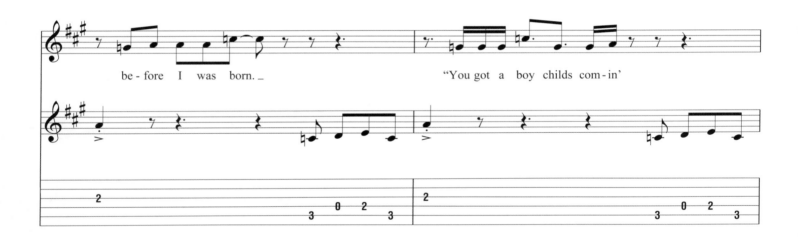

be - fore I was born. ___   "You got a boy childs com-in'

gon-na be a son-of-a-gun. ___   He gon-na make pret-ty wom-ens ___

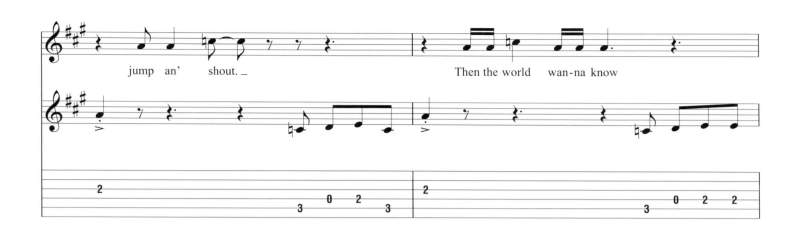

jump an' shout. _ Then the world wan-na know

Chorus

what this all a - bout?" _ But you know I'm here. __

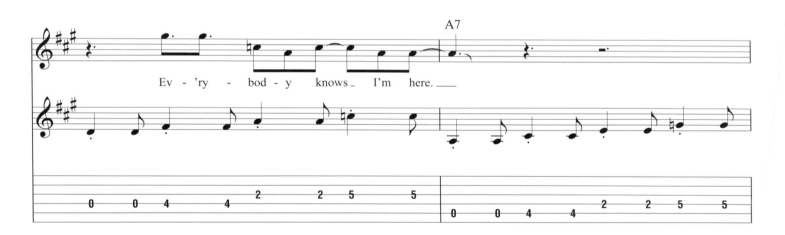

Ev - 'ry - bod - y knows_ I'm here. __

To Coda

Well, _ you know I'm the Hoo - chie Coo - chie Man, _

ev - 'ry-bod - y knows I'm here. ____

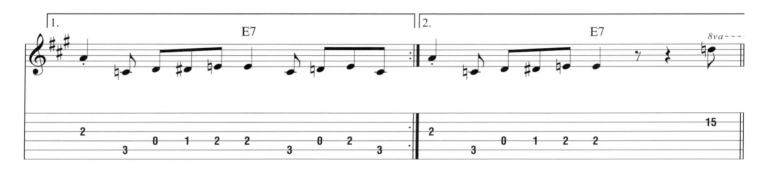

Guitar Solo

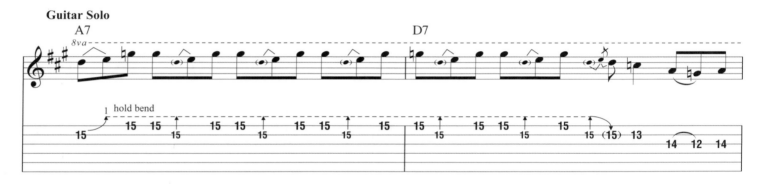

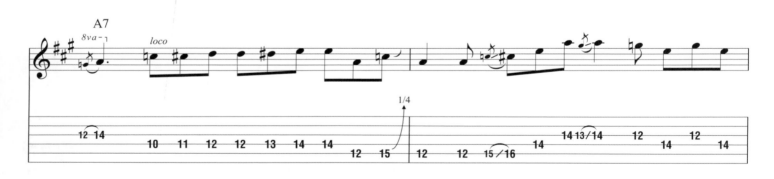

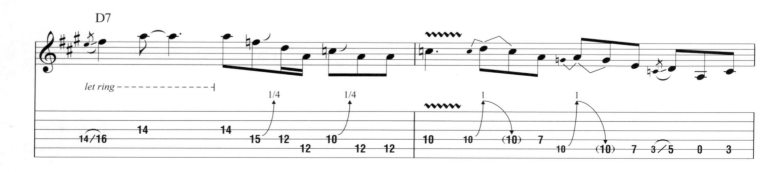

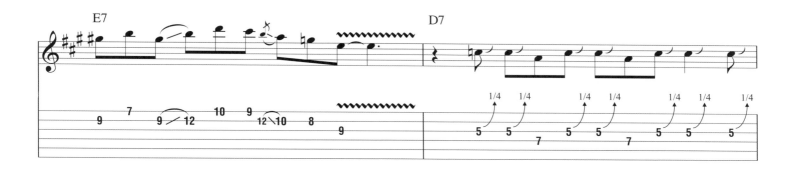

D.S. al Coda

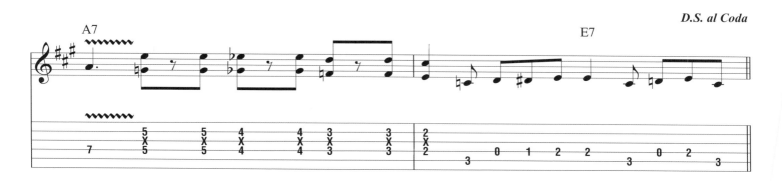

Coda

the whole _ round world knows I'm here.

Additional Lyrics

2. I got a black cat bone,
   I got a mojo too.
   I got the John the Conquerroot,
   I'm gonna mess with you.
   I'm gonna make you girls
   Lead me by my hand.
   Then the world'll know
   I'm the Hoochie Coochie man.

3. On the seventh hour,
   On the seventh day,
   On the seventh month,
   The seventh doctor say,
   "You were born for good luck,
   And that you'll see."
   I got seven hundred dollars,
   Don't you mess with me.

If You Love Me Like You Say

Words and Music by Little Johnny Taylor

Open Em tuning, up 1/2 step, Capo VII:
(low to high) F-C-F-A♭-C-F

*Symbols in parentheses represent chord names respective to capoed guitar.
Symbols above represent actual sounding chords. Capoed fret is "0" in tab.

Well, I ain't no fool. ___ I'm cool, ___ I know the

rule. ___

Guitar Solo

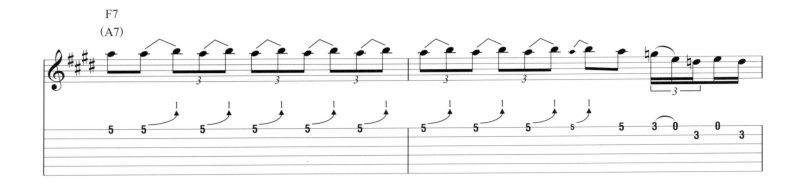

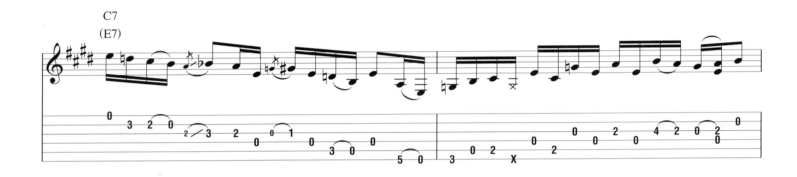

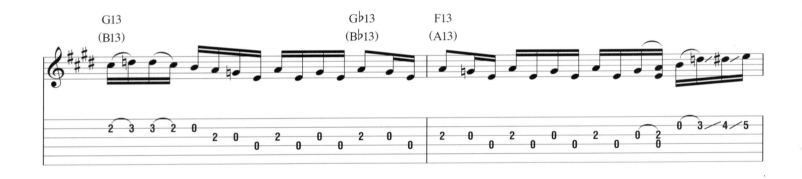

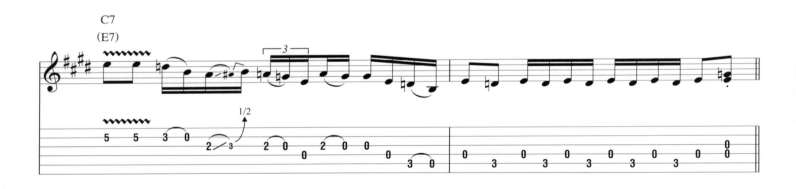

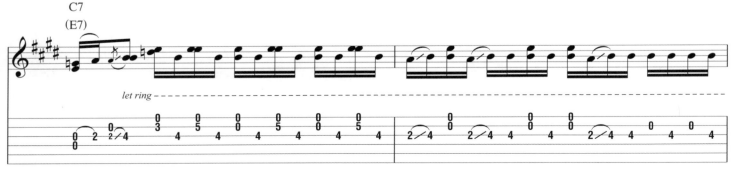

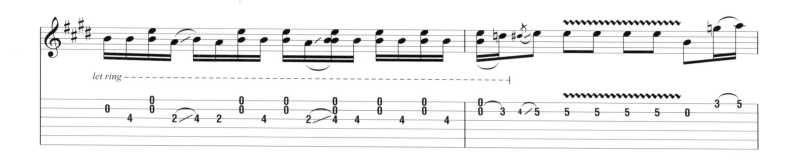

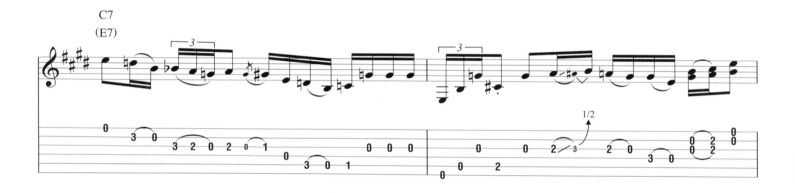

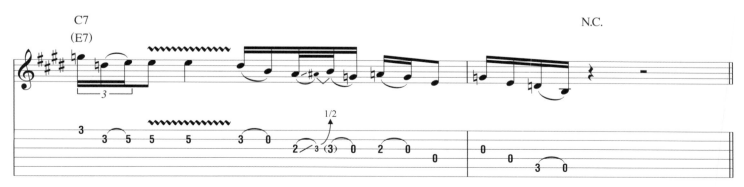

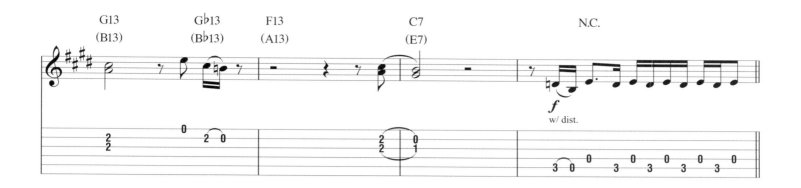

Guitar Solo

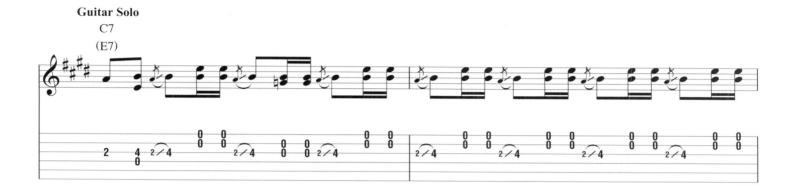

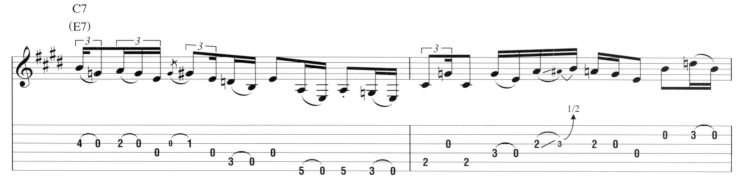

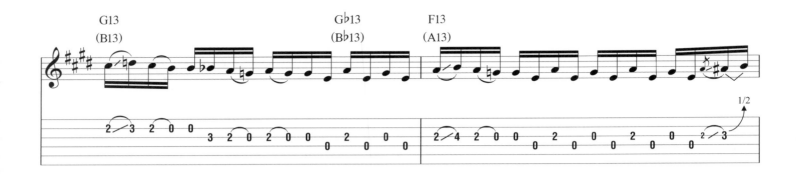

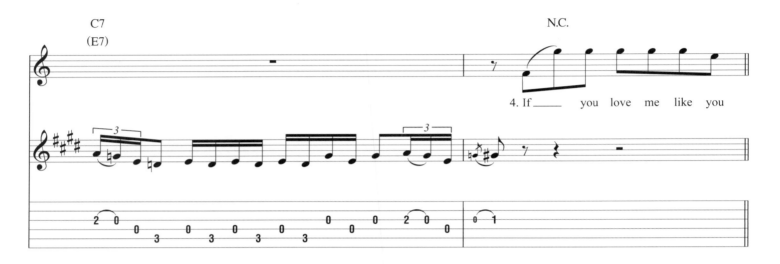

4. If ____ you love me like you

Verse

say, yeah, __ yeah, __ yeah, why you treat me like you ____ do?

w/ slight dist.

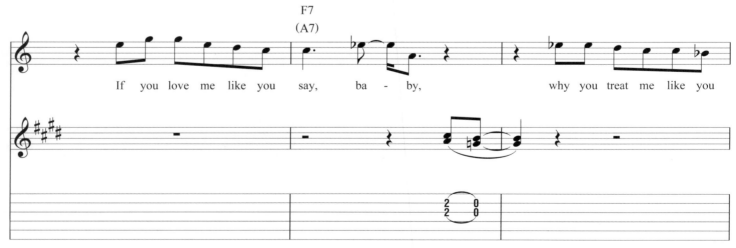

If you love me like you say, ba - by, why you treat me like you

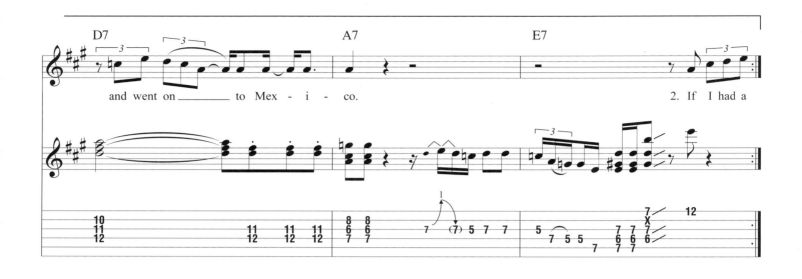

and went on _____ to Mex - i - co.   2. If I had a

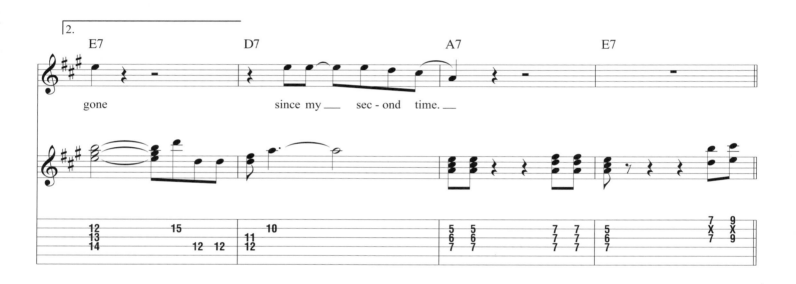

gone   since my ___ sec - ond time. ___

Guitar Solo

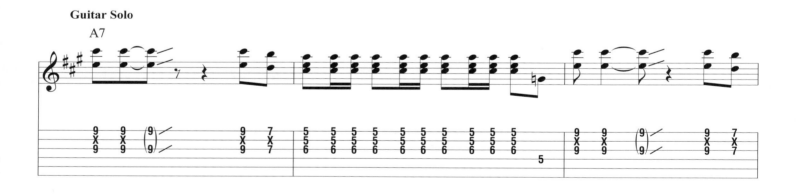

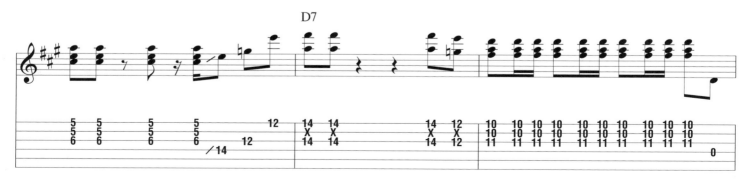

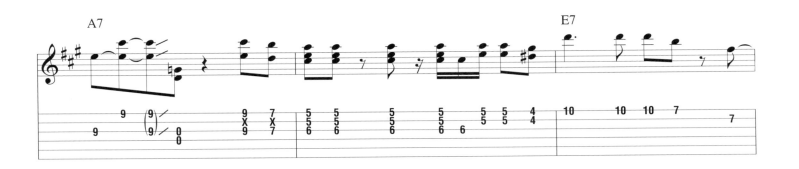

D.S. al Coda 1

3. I should have

Coda 1

fool - in' with you, ba - by, I let you put me on the ___ kill - ing

D.S. al Coda 2

floor.

4. God knows ___

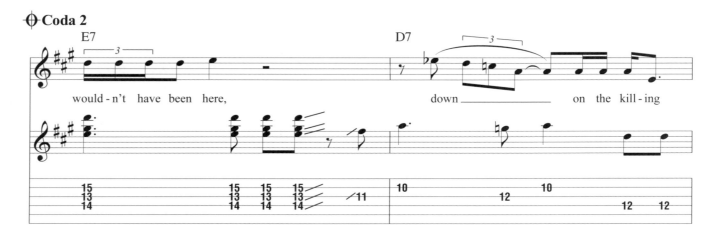

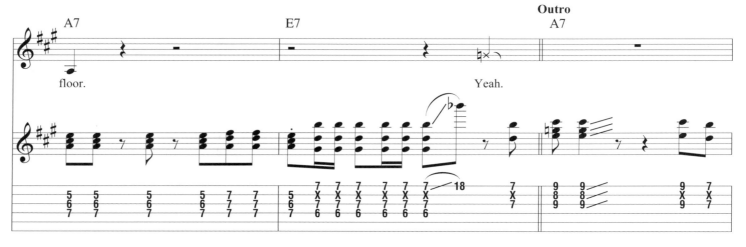

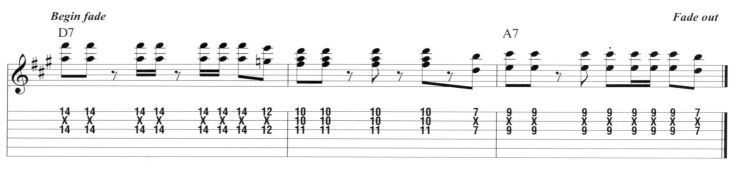

Additional Lyrics

2. If I had a followed my first mind,
   If I had a followed my first mind,
   I'd a been gone since my second time.

3. I should have went on when my friend come from Mexico at me.
   I should have went on when my friend come from Mexico at me.
   But now I'm foolin' with you, baby, I let you put me on the killing floor.

4. God knows I should have been gone.
   God knows I should have been gone.
   Then I wouldn't have been here, down on the killing floor.

Let Me Love You Baby

Words and Music by Willie Dixon

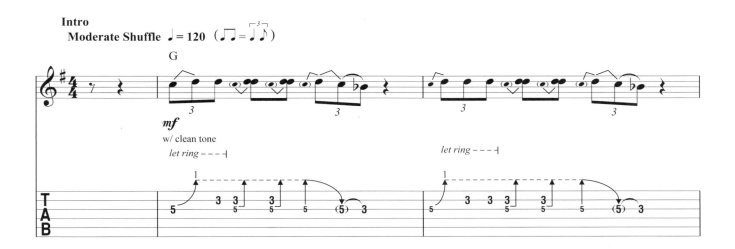

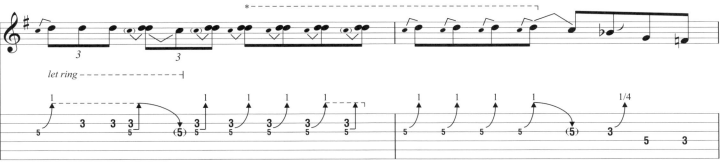

*Played as even eighth notes.

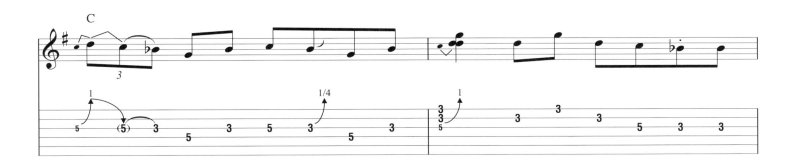

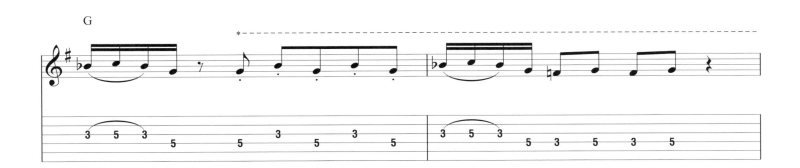

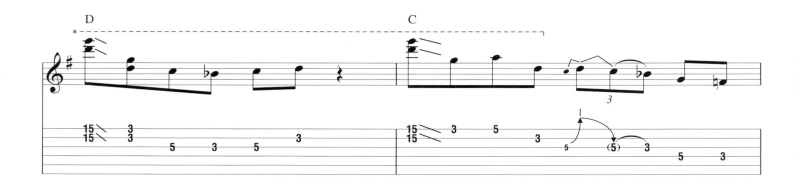

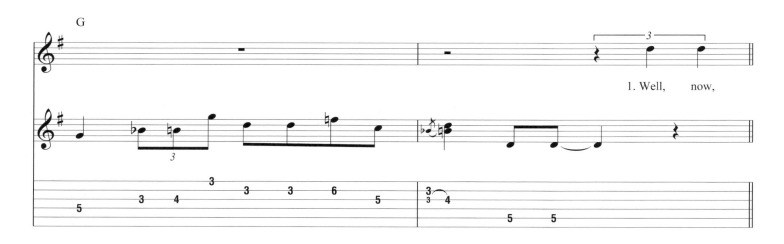

1. Well,   now,

% Verse

oo,   whee, ba - by, oo, I de - clare   you sure __ look fine. _____
2., 4. *See additional lyrics*

sim.

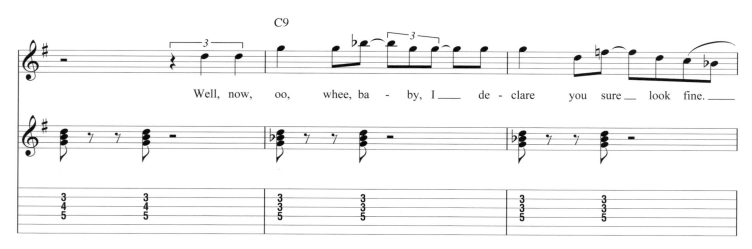

Well,   now,   oo,   whee, ba - by, I ___ de - clare   you sure __ look fine. ___

Well, a girl like you ___ will make, a,

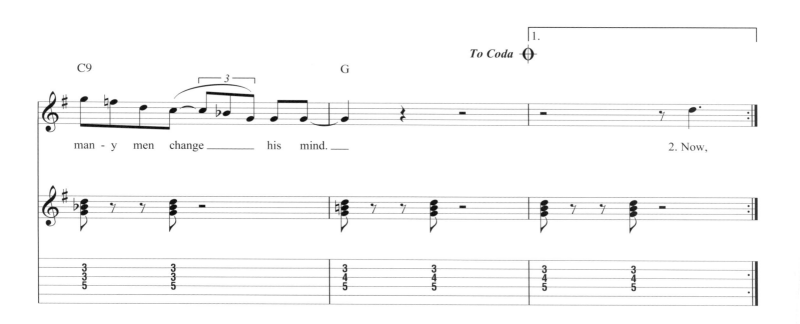

man - y men change ___ his mind. ___

To Coda

1.

2. Now,

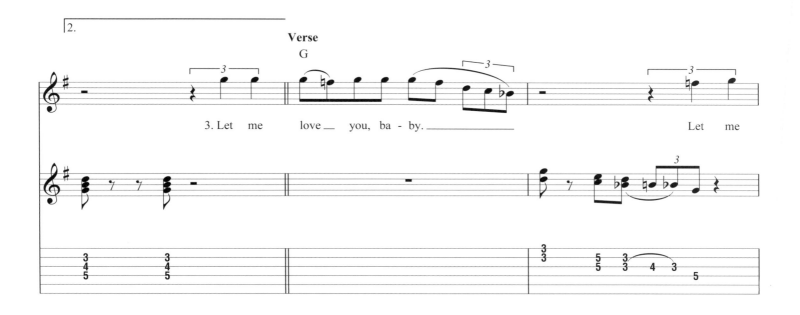

2.

Verse

3. Let me love ___ you, ba - by. ___

Let me

love — you, ba - by. _____   Whoa, — let me   love — you, ba   -   by.

Yes, — let me   love — you, babe. _____   Let me

love   you, ba   -   by, till your   good love   drives _____ me   cra   -   zy.

Guitar Solo

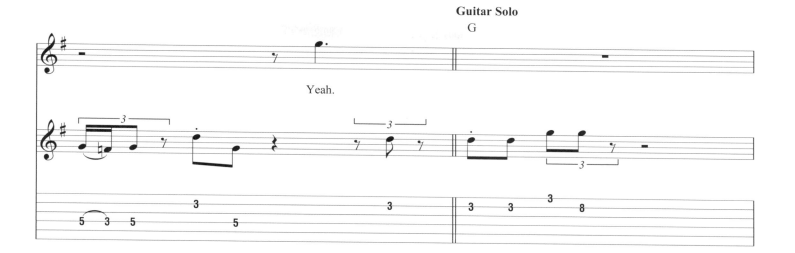

Yeah.

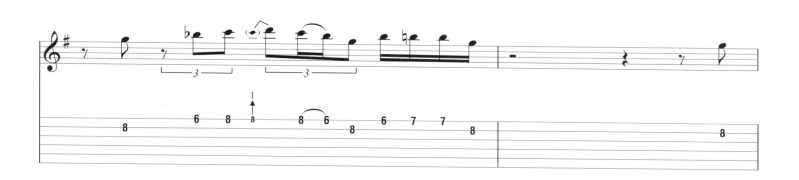

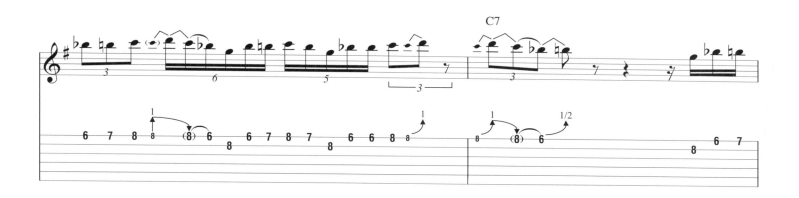

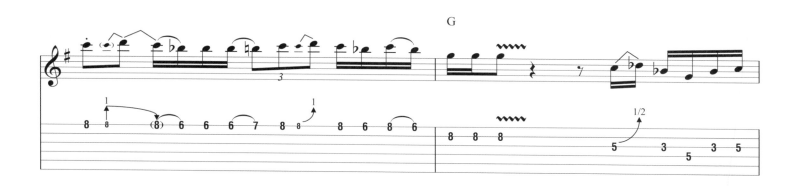

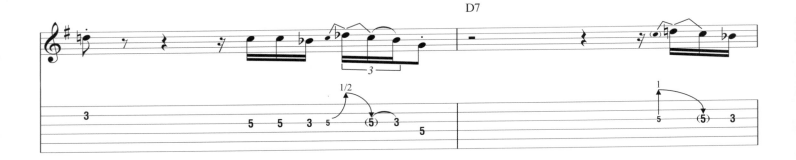

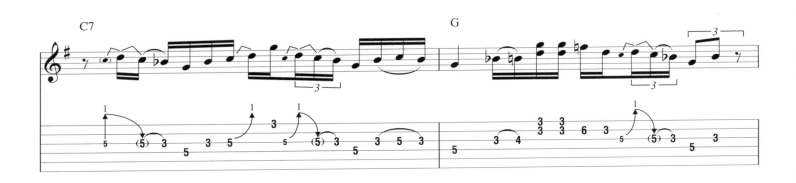

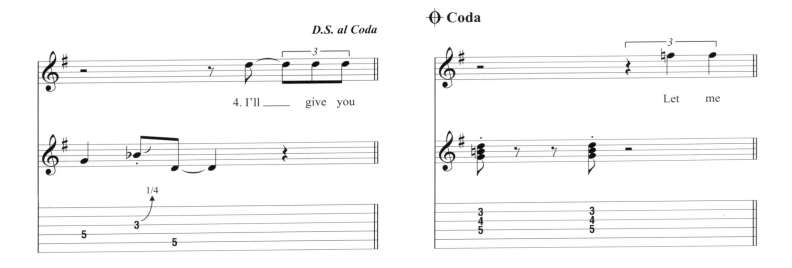

Outro

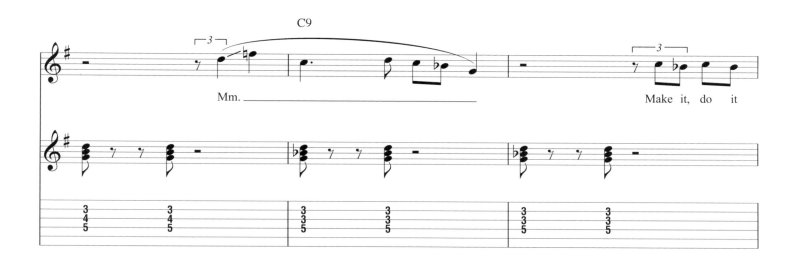

Mm. _____ Make it, do it

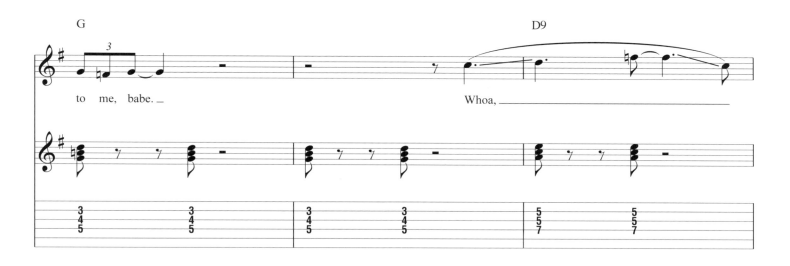

to me, babe. _ Whoa, _____

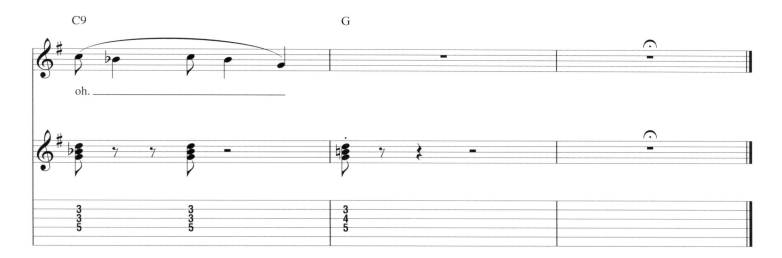

oh. _____

Additional Lyrics

2. Now, baby, when you walk, you know you shake like a willow tree.
   Now, baby, when you walk, you know you shake like a willow tree.
   Well, a girl like you I would love to make a fool of me.

4. I'll give you all I own just for a little bit of your love.
   I'll give you all I own just for a little bit of your love.
   Since I met you, baby, that's all I've been livin' for.

Messin' with the Kid

Words and Music by Mel London

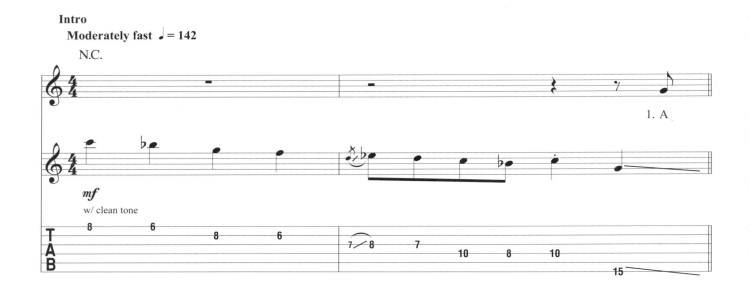

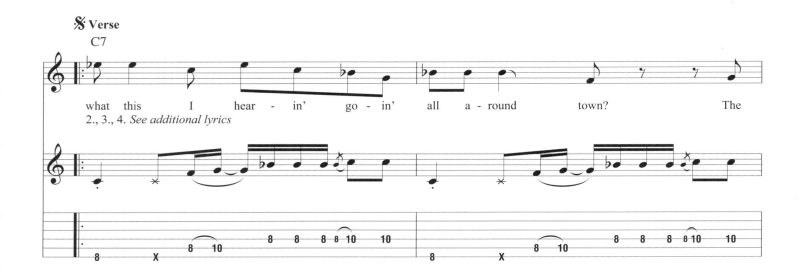

what this I hear-in' go-in' all a-round town? The
2., 3., 4. See additional lyrics

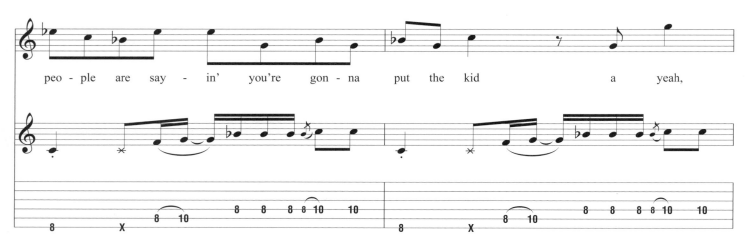

peo-ple are say-in' you're gon-na put the kid a yeah,

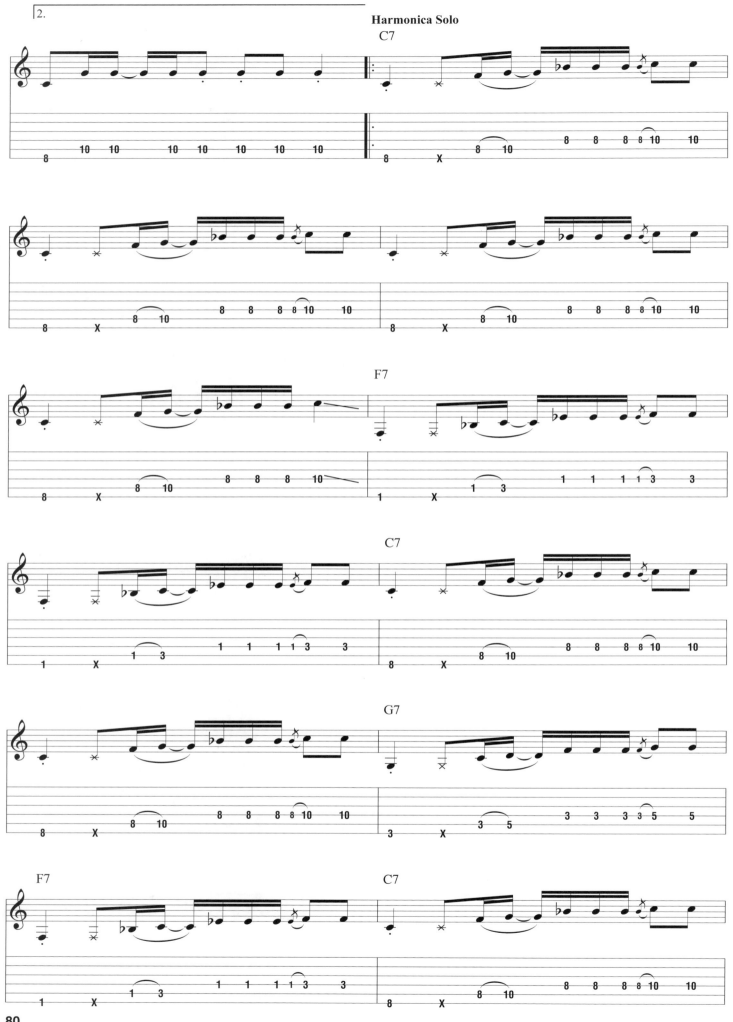

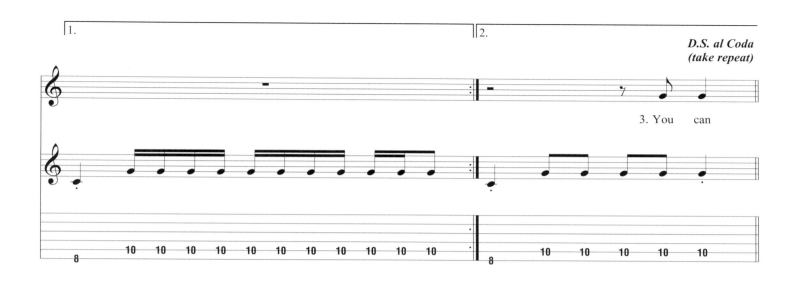

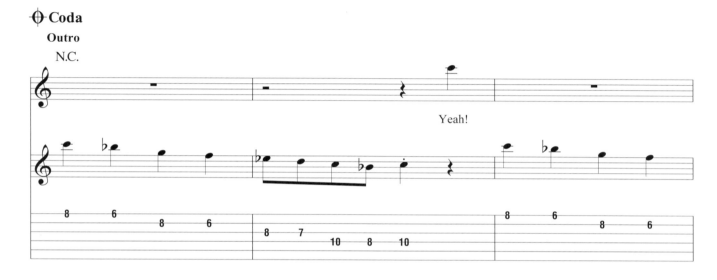

Additional Lyrics

2. You know the kid's no child, and I don't play. I says what I mean, I mean what I say.
   But oh, yeah, yeah, yeah, yeah. Oh, look at what you did.
   You can call it what you want, I call it messin' with the kid. Hey, look a here.

3. You can tell me you love me, you tell me a lie, but I love you baby till I die.
   But oh, no. Oh, look at what you did.
   You can call it what you want, I call it messin' with the kid.

4. We're gonna take the kid's car and drive around town, and tell ev'rybody you're, Lord, puttin' him down.
   But oh, yeah, yeah, yeah, yeah. Oh, look at what you did.
   You can call it what you want, I call it messin' with the...

(They Call It) Stormy Monday
(Stormy Monday Blues)
Words and Music by Aaron "T-Bone" Walker

1. They call it storm-y Mon-day, but Tues-day's just as bad.

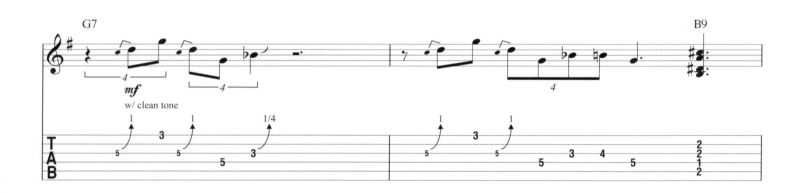

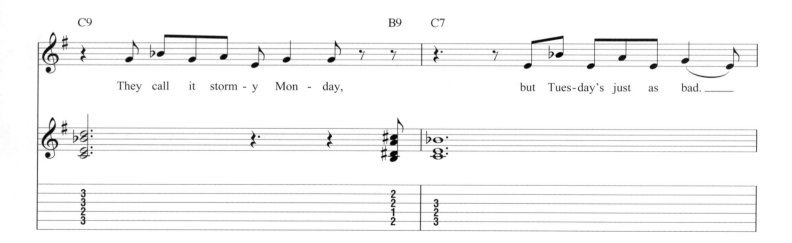

They call it storm-y Mon-day, but Tues-day's just as bad. ___

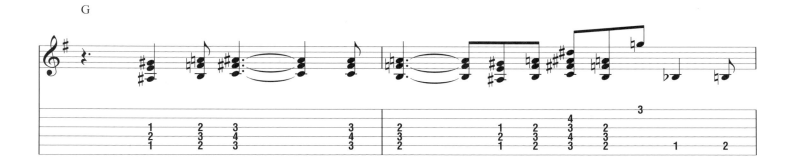

Wednes - day's worse, _ and _ Thurs - day's al - so sad. _

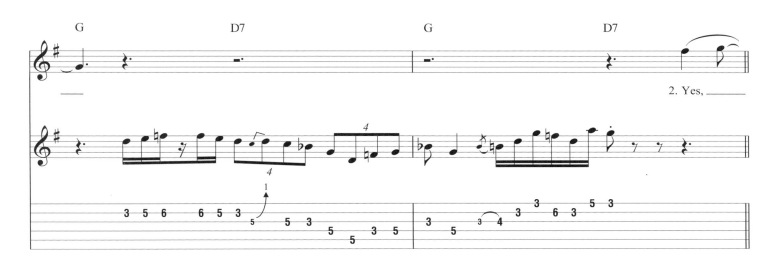

2. Yes, _____

Verse

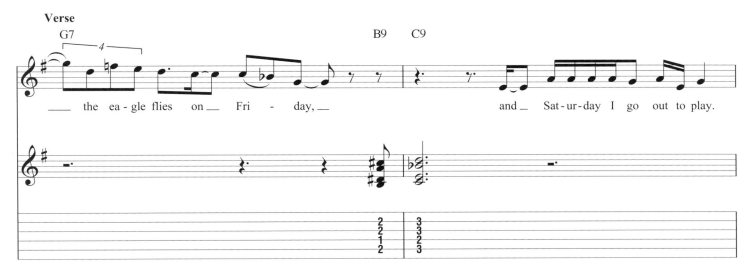

_ the ea - gle flies on _ Fri - day, _ and _ Sat - ur - day I go out to play.

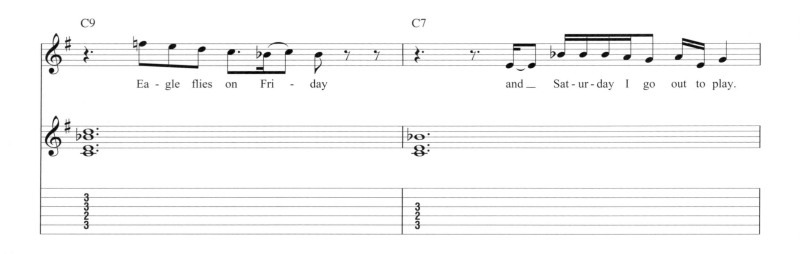

Ea - gle flies on Fri - day   and __ Sat - ur - day I go out to play.

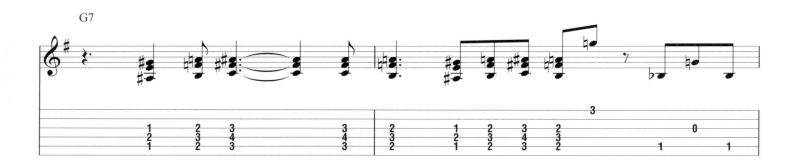

Sun-day I go to church,   then I ___ kneel ___ down and

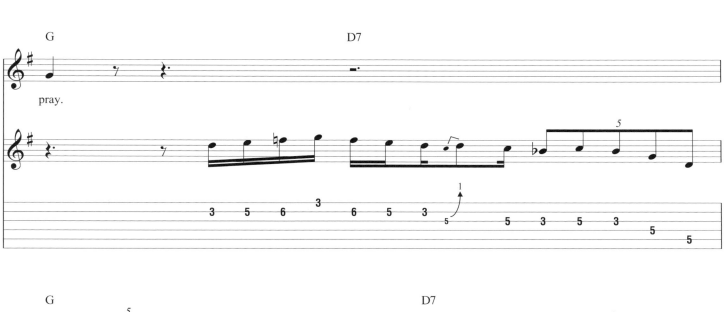

pray.

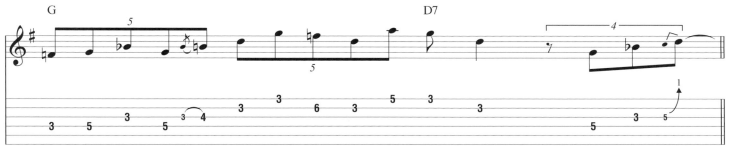

Guitar Solo

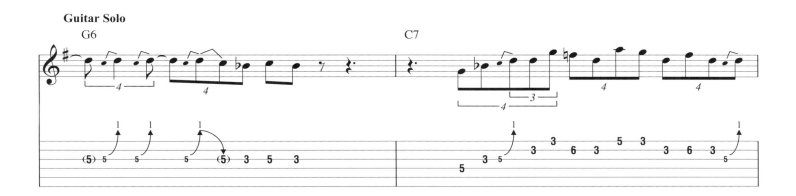

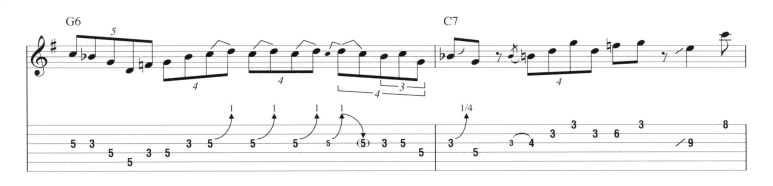

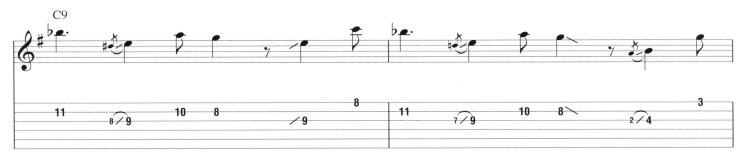

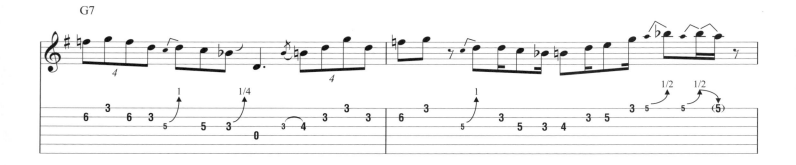

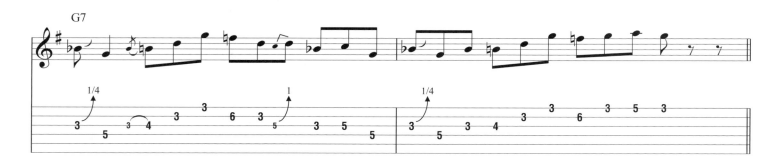

Verse

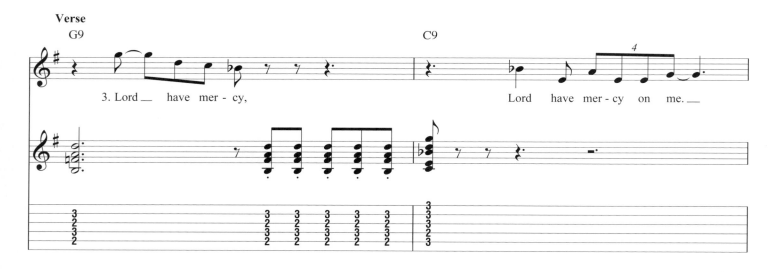

3. Lord __ have mer - cy,   Lord   have mer - cy on   me. __

Sweet Home Chicago

Words and Music by Robert Johnson

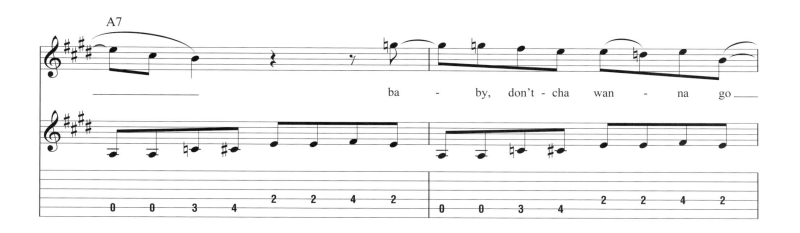

ba - by, don't - cha wan - na go

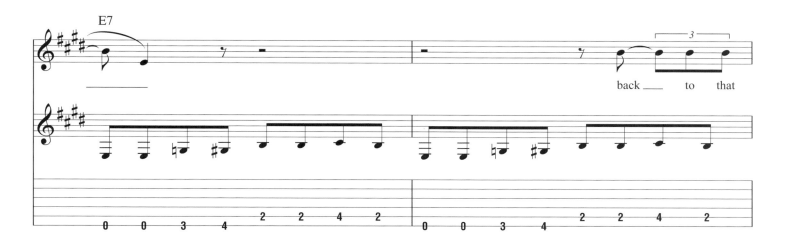

back to that

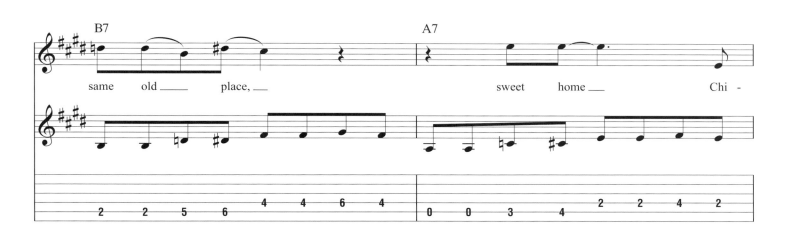

same old place, sweet home Chi -

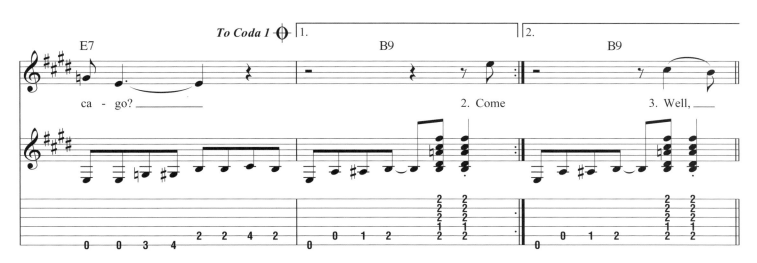

ca - go? 2. Come 3. Well,

D.S.S. al Coda 2

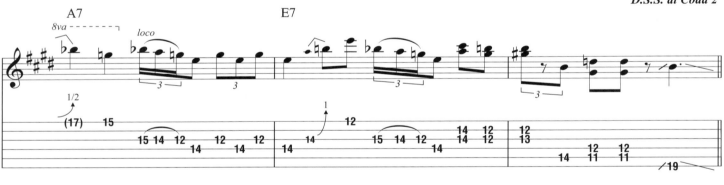

⊕ Coda 2

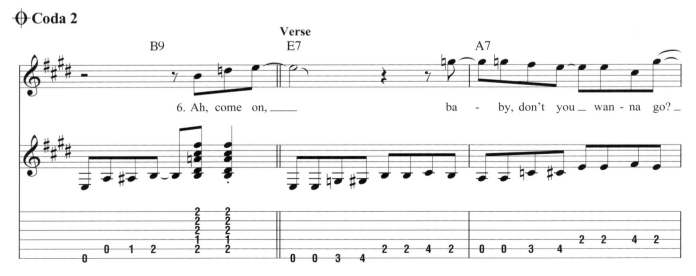

6. Ah, come on, _____ ba - by, don't you _ wan - na go? _

Pride and Joy

Written by Stevie Ray Vaughan

Tune down 1/2 step:
(low to high) Eb-Ab-Db-Gb-Bb-Eb

Verse

3. Yeah, I love my la-dy, to be long and ___ lean. ___

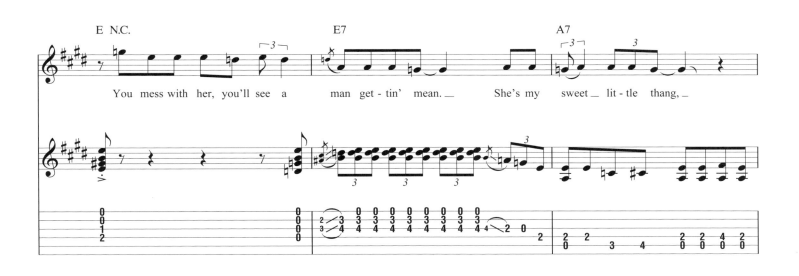

You mess with her, you'll see a man get-tin' mean. ___ She's my sweet ___ lit-tle thang, ___

she's my pride and joy. ___ She's my

sweet ___ lit-tle ba - by, I'm ___ her ___ lit - tle lov - er boy. ___

Guitar Solo

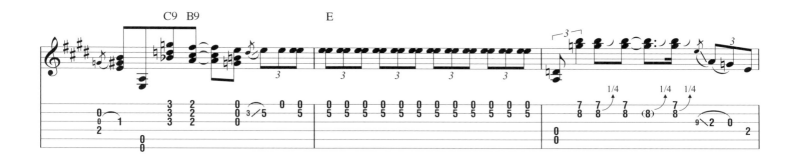

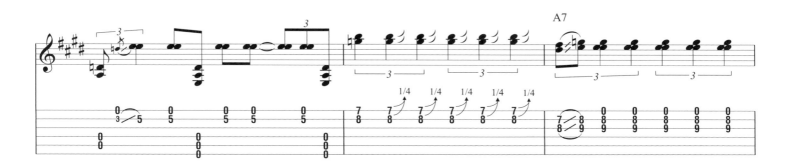

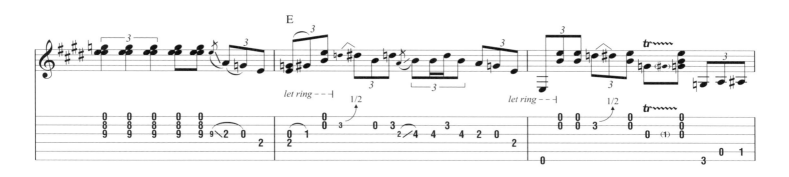

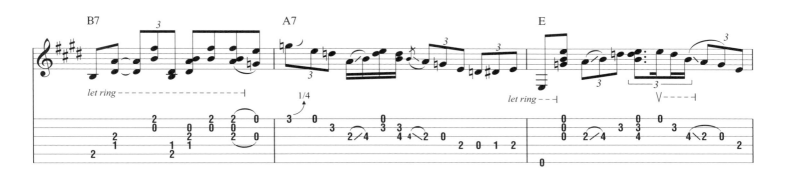

Verse

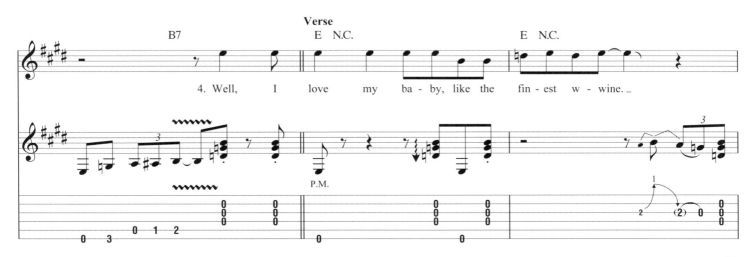

4. Well, I love my ba - by, like the fin - est w - wine. _

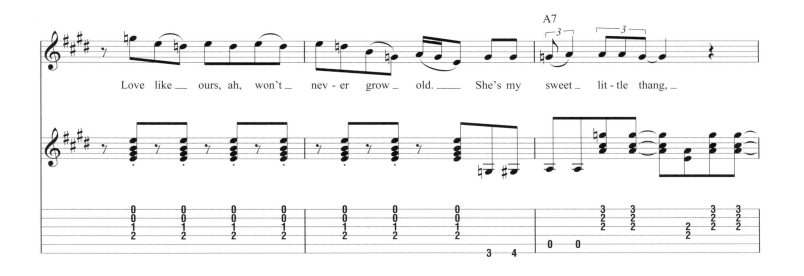

Love like ___ ours, ah, won't ___ nev - er grow ___ old. ___ She's my sweet ___ lit - tle thang, ___

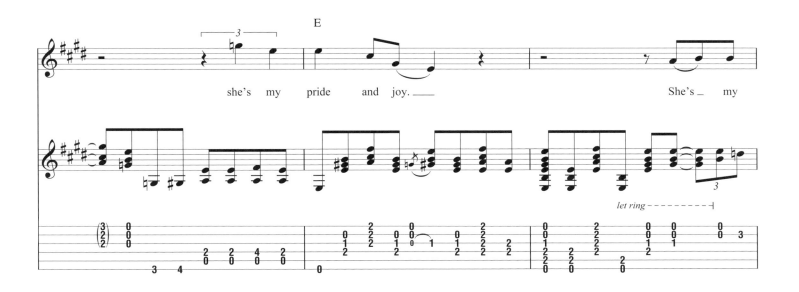

she's my pride and joy. ___ She's ___ my

sweet lit - tle ba - by, I'm ___ her lit - tle lov - er boy. ___

Guitar Solo

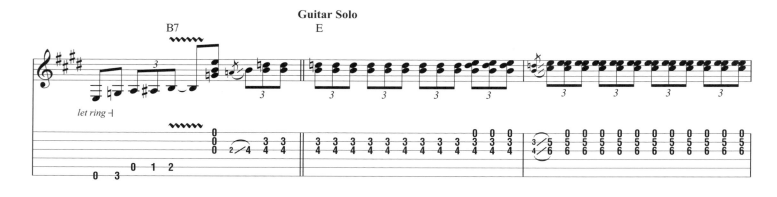

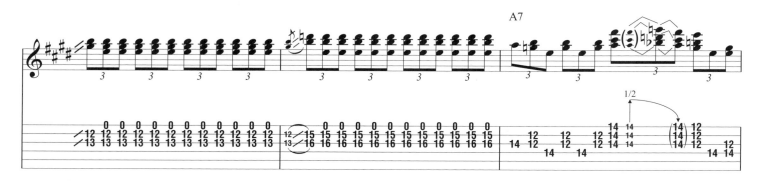

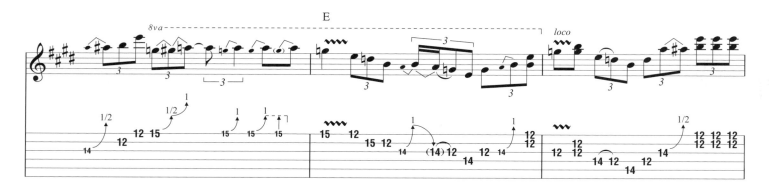

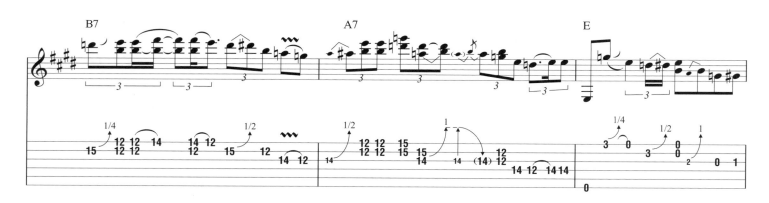

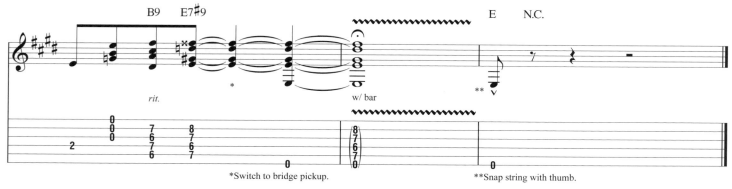

*Switch to bridge pickup.

**Snap string with thumb.

DELUXE GUITAR PLAY-ALONG

AUDIO ACCESS INCLUDED 🔊

The Deluxe Guitar Play-Along series will help you play songs faster than ever before! Accurate, easy-to-read guitar tab and professional, customizable audio for 15 songs. The interactive, online audio interface includes tempo/pitch control, looping, buttons to turn instruments on or off, and guitar tab with follow-along marker. The price of each book includes access to audio tracks online using the unique code inside. The tracks can also be downloaded and played offline. Now including PLAYBACK+, a multi-functional audio player that allows you to slow down audio, change pitch, set loop points, and pan left or right – available exclusively from Hal Leonard.

1. TOP ROCK HITS
Basket Case • Black Hole Sun • Come As You Are • Do I Wanna Know? • Gold on the Ceiling • Heaven • How You Remind Me • Kryptonite • No One Knows • Plush • The Pretender • Seven Nation Army • Smooth • Under the Bridge • Yellow Ledbetter.

00244758 Book/Online Audio $19.99

2. REALLY EASY SONGS
All the Small Things • Brain Stew • Californication • Free Fallin' • Helter Skelter • Hey Joe • Highway to Hell • Hurt (Quiet) • I Love Rock 'N Roll • Island in the Sun • Knockin' on Heaven's Door • La Bamba • Oh, Pretty Woman • Should I Stay or Should I Go • Smells Like Teen Spirit.

00244877 Book/Online Audio $19.99

3. ACOUSTIC SONGS
All Apologies • Banana Pancakes • Crash Into Me • Good Riddance (Time of Your Life) • Hallelujah • Hey There Delilah • Ho Hey • I Will Wait • I'm Yours • Iris • More Than Words • No Such Thing • Photograph • What I Got • Wonderwall.

00244709 Book/Online Audio $19.99

4. THE BEATLES
All My Loving • And I Love Her • Back in the U.S.S.R. • Don't Let Me Down • Get Back • A Hard Day's Night • Here Comes the Sun • I Will • In My Life • Let It Be • Michelle • Paperback Writer • Revolution • While My Guitar Gently Weeps • Yesterday.

00244968 Book/Online Audio $19.99

5. BLUES STANDARDS
Baby, What You Want Me to Do • Crosscut Saw • Double Trouble • Every Day I Have the Blues • Going Down • I'm Tore Down • I'm Your Hoochie Coochie Man • If You Love Me Like You Say • Just Your Fool • Killing Floor • Let Me Love You Baby • Messin' with the Kid • Pride and Joy • (They Call It) Stormy Monday (Stormy Monday Blues) • Sweet Home Chicago.

00245090 Book/Online Audio $19.99

6. RED HOT CHILI PEPPERS
The Adventures of Rain Dance Maggie • Breaking the Girl • Can't Stop • Dani California • Dark Necessities • Give It Away • My Friends • Otherside • Road Trippin' • Scar Tissue • Snow (Hey Oh) • Suck My Kiss • Tell Me Baby • Under the Bridge • The Zephyr Song.

00245089 Book/Online Audio $19.99

7. CLASSIC ROCK
Baba O'Riley • Born to Be Wild • Comfortably Numb • Dream On • Fortunate Son • Heartbreaker • Hotel California • Jet Airliner • More Than a Feeling • Old Time Rock & Roll • Rhiannon • Runnin' Down a Dream • Start Me Up • Sultans of Swing • Sweet Home Alabama.

00248381 Book/Online Audio $19.99

8. OZZY OSBOURNE
Bark at the Moon • Close My Eyes Forever • Crazy Train • Dreamer • Goodbye to Romance • I Don't Know • I Don't Wanna Stop • Mama, I'm Coming Home • Miracle Man • Mr. Crowley • No More Tears • Over the Mountain • Perry Mason • Rock 'N Roll Rebel • Shot in the Dark.

00248413 Book/Online Audio $19.99

9. ED SHEERAN
The A Team • All of the Stars • Castle on the Hill • Don't • Drunk • Galway Girl • Give Me Love • How Would You Feel (Paean) • I See Fire • Lego House • Make It Rain • Perfect • Photograph • Shape of You • Thinking Out Loud.

00248439 Book/Online Audio $19.99

10. CHRISTMAS SONGS
Blue Christmas • Christmas Time Is Here • Do You Hear What I Hear • Feliz Navidad • Have Yourself a Merry Little Christmas • I'll Be Home for Christmas • Let It Snow! Let It Snow! Let It Snow! • Little Saint Nick • Please Come Home for Christmas • Santa Baby • Santa Claus Is Comin' to Town • Sleigh Ride • Somewhere in My Memory • White Christmas • Winter Wonderland.

00278088 Book/Online Audio $19.99

HAL•LEONARD®

www.halleonard.com

1018
467

HAL•LEONARD® GUITAR PLAY-ALONG

AUDIO ACCESS INCLUDED

This series will help you play your favorite songs quickly and easily. Just follow the tab and listen to the audio to the hear how the guitar should sound, and then play along using the separate backing tracks. Audio files also include software to slow down the tempo without changing pitch. The melody and lyrics are included in the book so that you can sing or simply follow along.

INCLUDES TAB

VOL. 1 – ROCK	00699570 / $16.99	
VOL. 2 – ACOUSTIC	00699569 / $16.99	
VOL. 3 – HARD ROCK	00699573 / $17.99	
VOL. 4 – POP/ROCK	00699571 / $16.99	
VOL. 6 – '90S ROCK	00699572 / $16.99	
VOL. 7 – BLUES	00699575 / $17.99	
VOL. 8 – ROCK	00699585 / $16.99	
VOL. 9 – EASY ACOUSTIC SONGS	00151708 / $16.99	
VOL. 10 – ACOUSTIC	00699586 / $16.95	
VOL. 11 – EARLY ROCK	00699579 / $14.95	
VOL. 12 – POP/ROCK	00699587 / $14.95	
VOL. 13 – FOLK ROCK	00699581 / $16.99	
VOL. 14 – BLUES ROCK	00699582 / $16.99	
VOL. 15 – R&B	00699583 / $16.99	
VOL. 16 – JAZZ	00699584 / $15.95	
VOL. 17 – COUNTRY	00699588 / $16.99	
VOL. 18 – ACOUSTIC ROCK	00699577 / $15.95	
VOL. 19 – SOUL	00699578 / $15.99	
VOL. 20 – ROCKABILLY	00699580 / $16.99	
VOL. 21 – SANTANA	00174525 / $17.99	
VOL. 22 – CHRISTMAS	00699600 / $15.99	
VOL. 23 – SURF	00699635 / $15.99	
VOL. 24 – ERIC CLAPTON	00699649 / $17.99	
VOL. 25 – THE BEATLES	00198265 / $17.99	
VOL. 26 – ELVIS PRESLEY	00699643 / $16.99	
VOL. 27 – DAVID LEE ROTH	00699645 / $16.95	
VOL. 28 – GREG KOCH	00699646 / $16.99	
VOL. 29 – BOB SEGER	00699647 / $15.99	
VOL. 30 – KISS	00699644 / $16.99	
VOL. 32 – THE OFFSPRING	00699653 / $14.95	
VOL. 33 – ACOUSTIC CLASSICS	00699656 / $17.99	
VOL. 34 – CLASSIC ROCK	00699658 / $17.99	
VOL. 35 – HAIR METAL	00699660 / $17.99	
VOL. 36 – SOUTHERN ROCK	00699661 / $17.99	
VOL. 37 – ACOUSTIC UNPLUGGED	00699662 / $22.99	
VOL. 38 – BLUES	00699663 / $16.95	
VOL. 39 – '80S METAL	00699664 / $16.99	
VOL. 40 – INCUBUS	00699668 / $17.95	
VOL. 41 – ERIC CLAPTON	00699669 / $17.99	
VOL. 42 – COVER BAND HITS	00211597 / $16.99	
VOL. 43 – LYNYRD SKYNYRD	00699681 / $17.95	
VOL. 44 – JAZZ	00699689 / $16.99	
VOL. 45 – TV THEMES	00699718 / $14.95	
VOL. 46 – MAINSTREAM ROCK	00699722 / $16.95	
VOL. 47 – HENDRIX SMASH HITS	00699723 / $19.99	
VOL. 48 – AEROSMITH CLASSICS	00699724 / $17.99	
VOL. 49 – STEVIE RAY VAUGHAN	00699725 / $17.99	
VOL. 50 – VAN HALEN 1978-1984	00110269 / $17.99	
VOL. 51 – ALTERNATIVE '90S	00699727 / $14.99	
VOL. 52 – FUNK	00699728 / $15.99	
VOL. 53 – DISCO	00699729 / $14.99	
VOL. 54 – HEAVY METAL	00699730 / $15.99	
VOL. 55 – POP METAL	00699731 / $14.95	
VOL. 56 – FOO FIGHTERS	00699749 / $15.99	
VOL. 59 – CHET ATKINS	00702347 / $16.99	
VOL. 62 – CHRISTMAS CAROLS	00699798 / $12.95	
VOL. 63 – CREEDENCE CLEARWATER REVIVAL	00699802 / $16.99	
VOL. 64 – THE ULTIMATE OZZY OSBOURNE	00699803 / $17.99	
VOL. 66 – THE ROLLING STONES	00699807 / $17.99	
VOL. 67 – BLACK SABBATH	00699808 / $16.99	
VOL. 68 – PINK FLOYD – DARK SIDE OF THE MOON	00699809 / $16.99	

VOL. 69 – ACOUSTIC FAVORITES	00699810 / $16.99	
VOL. 70 – OZZY OSBOURNE	00699805 / $16.99	
VOL. 73 – BLUESY ROCK	00699829 / $16.99	
VOL. 74 – SIMPLE STRUMMING SONGS	00151706 / $19.99	
VOL. 75 – TOM PETTY	00699882 / $16.99	
VOL. 76 – COUNTRY HITS	00699884 / $16.99	
VOL. 77 – BLUEGRASS	00699910 / $15.99	
VOL. 78 – NIRVANA	00700132 / $16.99	
VOL. 79 – NEIL YOUNG	00700133 / $24.99	
VOL. 80 – ACOUSTIC ANTHOLOGY	00700175 / $19.95	
VOL. 81 – ROCK ANTHOLOGY	00700176 / $22.99	
VOL. 82 – EASY SONGS	00700177 / $14.99	
VOL. 83 – THREE CHORD SONGS	00700178 / $16.99	
VOL. 84 – STEELY DAN	00700200 / $16.99	
VOL. 85 – THE POLICE	00700269 / $16.99	
VOL. 86 – BOSTON	00700465 / $16.99	
VOL. 87 – ACOUSTIC WOMEN	00700763 / $14.99	
VOL. 89 – REGGAE	00700468 / $15.99	
VOL. 90 – CLASSICAL POP	00700469 / $14.99	
VOL. 91 – BLUES INSTRUMENTALS	00700505 / $15.99	
VOL. 92 – EARLY ROCK INSTRUMENTALS	00700506 / $15.99	
VOL. 93 – ROCK INSTRUMENTALS	00700507 / $16.99	
VOL. 94 – SLOW BLUES	00700508 / $16.99	
VOL. 95 – BLUES CLASSICS	00700509 / $15.99	
VOL. 96 – BEST COUNTRY HITS	00211615 / $16.99	
VOL. 97 – CHRISTMAS CLASSICS	00236542 / $14.99	
VOL. 99 – ZZ TOP	00700762 / $16.99	
VOL. 100 – B.B. KING	00700466 / $16.99	
VOL. 101 – SONGS FOR BEGINNERS	00701917 / $14.99	
VOL. 102 – CLASSIC PUNK	00700769 / $14.99	
VOL. 103 – SWITCHFOOT	00700773 / $16.99	
VOL. 104 – DUANE ALLMAN	00700846 / $16.99	
VOL. 105 – LATIN	00700939 / $16.99	
VOL. 106 – WEEZER	00700958 / $14.99	
VOL. 107 – CREAM	00701069 / $16.99	
VOL. 108 – THE WHO	00701053 / $16.99	
VOL. 109 – STEVE MILLER	00701054 / $17.99	
VOL. 110 – SLIDE GUITAR HITS	00701055 / $16.99	
VOL. 111 – JOHN MELLENCAMP	00701056 / $14.99	
VOL. 112 – QUEEN	00701052 / $16.99	
VOL. 113 – JIM CROCE	00701058 / $16.99	
VOL. 114 – BON JOVI	00701060 / $16.99	
VOL. 115 – JOHNNY CASH	00701070 / $16.99	
VOL. 116 – THE VENTURES	00701124 / $16.99	
VOL. 117 – BRAD PAISLEY	00701224 / $16.99	
VOL. 118 – ERIC JOHNSON	00701353 / $16.99	
VOL. 119 – AC/DC CLASSICS	00701356 / $17.99	
VOL. 120 – PROGRESSIVE ROCK	00701457 / $14.99	
VOL. 121 – U2	00701508 / $16.99	
VOL. 122 – CROSBY, STILLS & NASH	00701610 / $16.99	
VOL. 123 – LENNON & MCCARTNEY ACOUSTIC	00701614 / $16.99	
VOL. 125 – JEFF BECK	00701687 / $16.99	
VOL. 126 – BOB MARLEY	00701701 / $16.99	
VOL. 127 – 1970S ROCK	00701739 / $16.99	
VOL. 128 – 1960S ROCK	00701740 / $14.99	
VOL. 129 – MEGADETH	00701741 / $16.99	
VOL. 130 – IRON MAIDEN	00701742 / $17.99	
VOL. 131 – 1990S ROCK	00701743 / $14.99	
VOL. 132 – COUNTRY ROCK	00701757 / $15.99	
VOL. 133 – TAYLOR SWIFT	00701894 / $16.99	
VOL. 134 – AVENGED SEVENFOLD	00701906 / $16.99	
VOL. 135 – MINOR BLUES	00151350 / $17.99	
VOL. 136 – GUITAR THEMES	00701922 / $14.99	

VOL. 137 – IRISH TUNES	00701966 / $15.99	
VOL. 138 – BLUEGRASS CLASSICS	00701967 / $16.99	
VOL. 139 – GARY MOORE	00702370 / $16.99	
VOL. 140 – MORE STEVIE RAY VAUGHAN	00702396 / $17.99	
VOL. 141 – ACOUSTIC HITS	00702401 / $16.99	
VOL. 142 – GEORGE HARRISON	00237697 / $17.99	
VOL. 143 – SLASH	00702425 / $19.99	
VOL. 144 – DJANGO REINHARDT	00702531 / $16.99	
VOL. 145 – DEF LEPPARD	00702532 / $17.99	
VOL. 146 – ROBERT JOHNSON	00702533 / $16.99	
VOL. 147 – SIMON & GARFUNKEL	14041591 / $16.99	
VOL. 148 – BOB DYLAN	14041592 / $16.99	
VOL. 149 – AC/DC HITS	14041593 / $17.99	
VOL. 150 – ZAKK WYLDE	02501717 / $16.99	
VOL. 151 – J.S. BACH	02501730 / $16.99	
VOL. 152 – JOE BONAMASSA	02501751 / $19.99	
VOL. 153 – RED HOT CHILI PEPPERS	00702990 / $19.99	
VOL. 155 – ERIC CLAPTON – FROM THE ALBUM UNPLUGGED	00703085 / $16.99	
VOL. 156 – SLAYER	00703770 / $17.99	
VOL. 157 – FLEETWOOD MAC	00101382 / $16.99	
VOL. 159 – WES MONTGOMERY	00102593 / $19.99	
VOL. 160 – T-BONE WALKER	00102641 / $16.99	
VOL. 161 – THE EAGLES – ACOUSTIC	00102659 / $17.99	
VOL. 162 – THE EAGLES HITS	00102667 / $17.99	
VOL. 163 – PANTERA	00103036 / $17.99	
VOL. 164 – VAN HALEN 1986-1995	00110270 / $17.99	
VOL. 165 – GREEN DAY	00210343 / $17.99	
VOL. 166 – MODERN BLUES	00700764 / $16.99	
VOL. 167 – DREAM THEATER	00111938 / $24.99	
VOL. 168 – KISS	00113421 / $16.99	
VOL. 169 – TAYLOR SWIFT	00115982 / $16.99	
VOL. 170 – THREE DAYS GRACE	00117337 / $16.99	
VOL. 171 – JAMES BROWN	00117420 / $16.99	
VOL. 172 – THE DOOBIE BROTHERS	00119670 / $16.99	
VOL. 173 – TRANS-SIBERIAN ORCHESTRA	00119907 / $19.99	
VOL. 174 – SCORPIONS	00122119 / $16.99	
VOL. 175 – MICHAEL SCHENKER	00122127 / $16.99	
VOL. 176 – BLUES BREAKERS WITH JOHN MAYALL & ERIC CLAPTON	00122132 / $19.99	
VOL. 177 – ALBERT KING	00123271 / $16.99	
VOL. 178 – JASON MRAZ	00124165 / $17.99	
VOL. 179 – RAMONES	00127073 / $16.99	
VOL. 180 – BRUNO MARS	00129706 / $16.99	
VOL. 181 – JACK JOHNSON	00129854 / $16.99	
VOL. 182 – SOUNDGARDEN	00138161 / $17.99	
VOL. 183 – BUDDY GUY	00138240 / $17.99	
VOL. 184 – KENNY WAYNE SHEPHERD	00138258 / $17.99	
VOL. 185 – JOE SATRIANI	00139457 / $17.99	
VOL. 186 – GRATEFUL DEAD	00139459 / $17.99	
VOL. 187 – JOHN DENVER	00140839 / $17.99	
VOL. 188 – MÖTLEY CRÜE	00141145 / $17.99	
VOL. 189 – JOHN MAYER	00144350 / $17.99	
VOL. 191 – PINK FLOYD CLASSICS	00146164 / $17.99	
VOL. 192 – JUDAS PRIEST	00151352 / $17.99	
VOL. 195 – METALLICA: 1983-1988	00234291 / $19.99	

Prices, contents, and availability subject to change without notice.

Complete song lists available online.

HAL•LEONARD®
www.halleonard.com

0618
173